GREAT AMERICAN ◁ FOR
JAMES BEARD
AND JULIA CHILD,
WHO LIT THE LAMP
AND SHOWED US
THE WAY ▷ COOKING SCHOOLS

GREAT AMERICAN COOKING SCHOOLS

# Soups & Salads

## SANDI COOPER

ILLUSTRATED BY JOAN BLUME

**IRENA CHALMERS COOKBOOKS, INC.** • **NEW YORK**

*This book is dedicated to the two cooks who got me going . . . Irene, my mother, and Mary, my grandmother, and to the one cook who supports my ongoings or perhaps my goings-on . . . Steve, my husband.*

*For my children, Eric and Michael, who have tasted life with me, for my staff and my father, who are always there, and for Wilma, who keeps things flowing—*

*how could I have done it without all of you?*

IRENA CHALMERS COOKBOOKS, INC.

PUBLISHER
Irena Chalmers

*Managing Editor*
Jean Atcheson

*Sales and Marketing Director*
Diane J. Kidd

*Series Design*
Helene Berinsky

*Cover Design*
Milton Glaser
Karen Skelton, *Associate Designer*

*Cover Photography*
Matthew Klein

*Editor for this book*
Betsy Lawrence

*Typesetting*
Cosmos Press, New York

*Printing*
Lucas Litho, Inc., Baltimore

*Editorial Offices*
23 East 92nd Street
New York, NY 10028
(212) 289-3105

*Sales Offices*
P.O. Box 322
Brown Summit, NC 27214
(800) 334-8128

ISBN # 0-941034-13-5
© 1982 by Sandi Cooper. All rights reserved.
Printed and published in the United States of America
by Irena Chalmers Cookbooks, Inc.
LIBRARY OF CONGRESS
CATALOG CARD NO.: 81-70441
    Cooper, Sandi.
       Soups & salads.

    New York, N.Y.: Chalmers, Irena Cookbooks, Inc.
84 p.
8110                811007
EDCBA65432        695/14

# Contents

## *Salads*

# About the Author

To have come to this time in my life as a cooking school teacher should never have surprised any of us. I received my degree in early childhood education, designed toys for Fisher-Price—and I cooked.

Even as a newlywed, I found that the food I served at dinner parties was always a great success. I had grown up in a household where food was wonderful and nutritious and every now and then a little offbeat—at least for those times. My grandmother's soups had no rivals and my mother's delicate hand produced quiche before it was fashionable. While I occasionally yearned for macaroni and cheese with ketchup, I respected the women in my life for the magic they created in the kitchen. For each one, the giving of a recipe was a gift of love. I hope I have come away with much of the same attitude.

In 1976, after many years of teaching cooking at the "Y," many years of greeting young women with baskets on their arms getting off trains to come to my private cooking classes, I opened my own "real" school, Complete Cuisine. Following my Fisher-Price experience, I set out to create an environment that was both secure for learning and fun to work in. My goal was to fill it with the toys of adulthood. "Out of the fire and into the frying pans," my husband quipped as I happily taught my fourth class of the week. I was loving every minute of it.

Gradually, the classes in Danish pastry in Copenhagen, the hours being "polished" at the Cordon Bleu in London, the thrilling kitchens of the Wei-Chuan School in Taipei all became part of the design, so that now my cooking school has become a 10,000-square-foot emporium for people who love food. The school has expanded with retail and wholesale bakeries that have brought culture (at least the kind of culture that "foodies" care about) to this part of the Midwest; the cookware shop carries only utensils that we really believe in. After all, if the tools you use make you confident in the kitchen, you'll come back; if a piece of poor equipment makes you feel frustrated, you won't. My little restaurant is growing in the hands of a pair of incredibly capable young chefs whose catering adventures have become the talk of the town. Beautiful foods (I hate the word "gourmet") are the backbone of my business. We sell bread flour and pastry flour, bulk unsalted butter and fresh eggs. I find fresh strawberries in December and sweet red peppers in January and load the shelves with olive oils and vinegars. And no matter how tired I am, my cooking school nurtures me.

I don't teach recipes to my students, I teach them theories; I teach them the miraculous science of foods. I've always felt that if you have learned the technique for something, and know what will happen and why, then a recipe is just a guideline. Nothing is as personal as taste buds and if I like two cloves of garlic and you like six, then the recipe tastes right to you only when it is made with six. Gods don't write cookbooks, only people do, yet sometimes the dogma found on the pages of a cookbook is astounding. Teaching confidence in the kitchen is my aim—making people happy about the hours they have to spend there and proud of the beautiful food they can prepare without feeling nervous. I will never forget the student who ran to Complete Cuisine, tears in her eyes, with her first perfect pie. She proudly offered it as a gift of thanks, but I didn't need the pie to know. The great big hug said it.

All the years of developmental psychology in college certainly never went to waste. "Cook until done," I always answered the worried student who asked, "How long?" "The smell will tell you and the look." With my arm around her we waited together and she learned. If I had just answered "Twenty minutes," she would never have known the joy of the just-done smell that causes your nostrils to quiver with anticipation, and of course I would never have let her burn it!

As a Certified Member and the second Vice President of the International Association of Cooking Schools, with all the diplomas hanging on the wall, it's apparent that my avocation has become my career. I have touched hundreds of students and they have all touched me. How lucky I am!

My students and I have shared inspired classes —and some not quite so. We have shared Jacques Pépin—the king of cooking teachers for me— Marcella Hazan, Simone Beck, Michael James, Paula Wolfert, Jane Freiman, Jack Lirio and Bernard Clayton. We have inspired each other—and so this book is born.

It was hard for me to write a book as exacting as books are, without allowing *you* to make some choices. The recipes herein work! And they taste good—to me. I invite you to experiment with herbs, to change the textures or the thickness, to make these recipes *your* recipes. I use very little salt in my cooking; I love the natural taste of food and very rarely have I given you an absolute measurement for salt or pepper. Taste it! Only you can tell when the dish is right for you.

# Equipment

The equipment required for turning out good soups and salads is really nothing more than one usually has in the kitchen. A choice of high-quality equipment, like high-quality food products, insures that your food adventures will have a good start. Insist that the equipment you choose does the job it was designed for.

**BLENDER:** Although almost obsolete since the advent of the food processor, the blender purees as well as ever. Use enough liquid, use small batches of food and be patient.

**CHEESECLOTH:** Choose a thin, loosely woven cotton cheesecloth whenever possible. Rinse well in hot soapy water before using to remove any soap or sizing. Cheesecloth makes a superb fine sieve when laid in a strainer. Use it when only the thinnest liquid must be removed from your dish. I also twist cheesecloth around cut lemons or oranges for squeezing seedless juice.

**COLANDER:** Like strainers and sieves, colanders are endlessly useful for straining things, holding things and rinsing things. It's great to have a variety of sizes available—a 5-quart colander is the one I use most often.

**CORKSCREW:** All good kitchens and dining rooms need a good corkscrew for opening wine bottles or olive oil bottles. I suggest using the type that has a small horizontal handle with two uneven-length prongs. Just wiggle the long prong down one side of the cork, work in the other, and, twisting gently, pull out the cork.

**CUTTING BOARD:** A good cutting board should be big enough for you to really spread out. I am still a proponent of wooden edge grain laminated boards, the thicker the better (1 inch is the minimum thickness for a good board). While many people have tried to convince me of the cleanliness of lucite, polywhatever or restaurant rubber, I stand unflinching in knowing that, if I'm going to scrape up something alien into my food, I'd rather it were wood than plastic. I wash my cutting board with hot water and a bit of bleach at least once a week to make sure it is clean. How to take care of a new cutting board? Just memorize this old wives' tale: oil it once a day for a week, once a week for a month and once a month for the rest of its life.

**FOOD MILL:** A food mill is a delightful, inexpensive gadget for passing and pressing food through a series of small holes. It doesn't do quite as fine a job as a food processor or a tamis, but it certainly does more than a passable one. Food mills with interchangeable discs have the added advantage of slicing (kind of), and grating and shredding, both of which they do well.

**FOOD PROCESSOR:** Never has a piece of equipment so revolutionized life in the kitchen. Not even Escoffier himself can claim to have had such an influence on so many cooks. While I still love doing many of the cooking processes by hand, the steel S blade's ability to puree and chop is sensational. Always puree in short on-and-off pulses, adding liquid as necessary. This keeps the food turning over so that all of it processes evenly. Don't be impatient, process small amounts at a time. I still slice by hand.

**GRATER:** Whether you prefer the old-fashioned box-shaped grater or the convenient hand-held rotary grater, this multipurpose cutting tool can grate many things, from horseradish to nutmeg. Perfect for grating cheese, whether hard or soft, potatoes or lemon peel, the sturdy old favorite works even in a power failure.

**KNIVES:** Chef's knives, paring knives, flexible slicers, brand names galore, made of carbon steel, high-carbon molybdenum, styled with full tang, rivets—the prospect is frightening. How do you know what kind of knives to buy?

Before you purchase a good knife, look carefully at the way it's made; examine the blade and the handle. The best knives are full tang construction, or one solid piece of metal that goes all the way through the handle and is then riveted in place. A full tang is always visible through the length of the handle. Not all knives require the strength of a solid tang—paring knives don't—only those that do a lot of heavy work. Pick up the knife before you decide. Don't worry about balancing it on your finger to check the balance, you don't cut with a knife on the end of your finger. Grasp it, feel how it feels to chop with. Chef's knives have a slightly rounded blade to aid in the chopping. Does the place where the knife rocks feel good to you? Is the handle a sure fit in *your* hand? Does the wide end of the knife, the heel (near where you grip) have enough protection so that you don't slide up onto the blade? Is there enough depth at the heel so that when you chop down firmly your knuckles clear the cutting board? If you've answered yes, then you've found the right chef's knife.

Choose one made of high carbon stainless steel, soft enough to be sharpened with ease, designed not to rust. All one really needs to own is an 8-inch or a 10-inch chef's knife and a paring knife. A good chef's knife should be long enough to slice bread as well as shred cabbage. Your paring knife shapes, decorates and pares. Choose these two carefully, and you will value them as you do your most comfortable pair of shoes.

**LADLE:** A series of long-handled ladles (usually stainless steel) with bowl capacities from 1 ounce to 12 ounces are most useful for emptying stockpots, adding liquids through food-processor feed tubes or for serving. Two-ounce, 4-ounce and 8-ounce are perfect.

**LEMON STRIPPER:** Flute a lemon, a zucchini, a cucumber or an orange—use your imagination. Place the notch against the top of your fruit or vegetable and zip downward to the base, removing a strip. Do this all around the piece of food, then slice it as you would normally and you have brightly striped slices of fruits and vegetables. The thin pieces of peel of at least some of the foods can be recycled; blanched and chopped for addition to salads or dropped into the stockpot. Unfortunately, I have yet to find a practical use for cucumber peels.

**LEMON ZESTER:** A clever tool which takes just the yellow, orange or green from the fruit (or vegetable), leaving behind the bitter part. Short strokes against the skin produce small bits; long strokes create tiny threads. Experiment with this tool to make garnishes.

**MANDOLINE:** The precursor of the food processor, a French mandoline slices and dices with alarming speed. Unfortunately, a mandoline is expensive as well as just a bit dangerous. If you own one, use a guard so your fingers don't get too close to the blade.

**MEASURING CUPS AND MEASURING SPOONS:** Although I do not own many of these, there are times when you will wish to be very accurate. A set of aluminum or stainless spoons, a set of cups measuring from 2 cups to ¼ cup for dry ingredients and a glass measuring cup of 2 or 4 cups for liquids should do the job. For true accuracy, level dry measures off at the rim with the flat of a knife. Read liquid measures at eye level.

**MELON BALLER:** Melon ballers come in a wide variety of shapes and sizes from ⅛-inch round to oval and ripple-shaped. A large selection is delightful but unnecessary for garnishing. (Imagine rippled ovals of precooked carrots garnishing a clear beef consommé.) The standard inexpensive double-headed melon baller (usually one side is ¾ inch in diameter and the other is 1¼ inch) is the most useful. Can't think of a use for your melon baller when melons are out of season? Try shaping potatoes or turnips, or use it to remove the seeds and the filament around the seeds from half an apple or pear. It makes a perfectly clean hemisphere and lends a very professional finish to the look of sliced apples or pears.

**MORTAR AND PESTLE:** A sturdy porcelain mortar, wide enough to allow you to really get in there and grind, along with a solid pestle to do the grinding, is what you need for grinding some herbs and spices. Avoid those cute, dainty little ones whose pestle is so small it can be grasped with only three fingers. One of the herbs I always grind this way is dry rosemary. While I want the essence of the whole leaves as opposed to buying the preground and dusty variety, I find the texture of the dry woody leaf interferes with my taste buds' appreciation of its taste. Well ground, it's perfect.

**PEPPERMILL:** Peppermills are essential equipment in the kitchen. Keep a dark one for black peppercorns, and a light one for white peppercorns. Choose one with a convenient action that holds enough peppercorns so you don't need to load it more than once a week, and make sure it has a nut on the top or bottom that allows you to adjust the coarseness of the grind.

**POTATO PEELER:** It doesn't matter which of the many shapes you choose, just make sure it feels comfortable in your hand. Buy inexpensive stainless steel ones; they won't get rusty, and you can throw them away when they get dull.

**SALAD SPINNER:** Rinse your lettuce quickly and place a moderate quantity in the basket portion of the spinner. Fill the bowl portion with cold water. Dunk the greens in their basket up and down in the cold water till they are absolutely clean. Change the water as often as necessary. Pour out the water, return the basket to the bowl, secure the lid and start to spin. The pressure of centrifugal force causes the water to be pulled out into the bowl. Once you have spun the basket several times, your lettuce will be dry. Layer the leaves with paper towels in a clean dish tub or a large bowl in the refrigerator; they will stay fresh and crisp for several days. A salad spinner works equally well with berries, but don't use the immersion method on raspberries or strawberries; it makes them too wet. A quick one or two dunkings in and out will do. This also works well for parsley and herbs.

**SCALES:** This is one of my favorite kitchen tools— so much more accurate than cups. Choose one that measures in ounces or in ounces and grams, choose a balance beam or a spring scale—they're all good. Just make sure that the dial is easy to read at counter height!

**SIEVES AND STRAINERS:** Owning a selection of fine, medium and coarse strainers ensures you will have just the right one for the job. And don't forget, a strainer works both ways. When you need to remove some stock from a pot that you are not ready to pour out yet, push in the strainer and ladle from within the strainer; everything you don't want stays behind in the pot.

**SKIMMER:** Sometimes a skimmer looks like a flat round spoon with a fine mesh for its bowl, sometimes it has a shallow round surface covered with holes. Both of these versions are used for skimming foam from stock. Just dip the skimmer into the stock, catch the foam on the edge of the pot and lift it out. Some skimmers are made of concentric wires; they do the same job as a slotted spoon. Always make sure the handle is securely attached to the rim . . . welded is best.

**SLOTTED SPOON:** A long-handled, preferably stainless steel spoon with holes or slots is required when you are removing whole foods from liquids which you wish to leave behind. Simply dip the spoon into your pot or bowl and lift out the pieces in turn. Don't forget to pause a moment to catch the drips over the pot.

**STEAMER:** The most handsome, as well as the most expensive steamer one can own is a multi-leveled bamboo steamer from the Orient. Its two covered layers allow you to steam two quantities of vegetables in a matter of minutes. Because of the open nature of the "floor" of each basket, the steaming process works in less time than is suggested in most cookbooks. Use your nose and taste for doneness. The bonus for using this type of steamer is the wonderful perfume of the wet bamboo. Be careful when removing these layers from the pan. Not only is the steam still trapped within, but the baskets themselves are hot.

The folding steamer basket opens its leaves to fit the size of your pan. Set over only an inch or two of water (but make sure the steamer sits *above* the water) and vegetables will steam to a firm, bright finish. This is a perfect way to cook vegetables that are to become Vegetables Vinaigrette or à la Grecque. Use this steamer in a covered pot.

To improvise a steamer, set a plate on a footed cake rack or a tunafish can with both ends removed, in a deep pot. Add water in the bottom and cover with a lid—voilà, a steamer that catches the juices. To avoid catching juices, add another cake rack on top of the plate.

**STOCKPOT:** A good stockpot is a large pot that distributes heat evenly, is light enough to handle when filled and heavy enough to simmer gently for many hours. Some are tall, some are squat, my own favorites are made of heavy aluminum and have a capacity of 12 quarts.

**WHISK:** Select a whisk the right size for the job. Choose a stainless steel one with lots of flexible wires (10-inch wires are my favorite) if you buy just one. Make sure the handle feels comfortable in your hand. Whisking a large mass is work and a whisk can help make the work easier.

# How to . . .

### Hard Cook an Egg

After I had been teaching for almost six years, I went off to the Cordon Bleu in London to get "polished." My first lesson was on how to hard cook an egg! This is what I learned in that lesson.

A perfect hard-cooked or hard-boiled egg is a thing of beauty. It has a firm but not rubbery white and a bright yellow yolk without a dark ring. Here's how to do it perfectly every time. Bring a large quantity of water to a rapid boil. Lower a room-temperature egg, on a metal spoon, into the pot. Touch down the bottom of the spoon first, thus absorbing the brunt of the shock of the heat. (To pierce or not to pierce your egg is your choice, but if you do, pierce the broad end.) Gently roll the egg off the spoon onto the pot bottom—do not let it bounce. Turn the heat down so that the eggs don't rumble; cook without a lid for exactly 12 minutes. Should one of the eggs crack in the water, add a little vinegar to instantly coagulate the escaping white. After 12 minutes, remove the eggs to cold running water; this stops the cooking and doesn't give that sulfuric dark ring a chance to form.

Gently crack the egg, all over, until it resembles ancient Chinese pottery. Leave it in the cold water until it is cool when held in the hand. Roll the egg gently between the palms of both hands and the shell should simply fall away. If you wish to keep the eggs warm after they're shelled, return them to hot tap water.

### Cook Rice

Here is a wonderful and foolproof way to cook rice. Bring two quarts of water to a boil with two teaspoons of salt. Add two cups rice and stir gently to separate the grains. Cook, just under the boil, for 12 minutes. Do not cover. Test for doneness by chewing on a grain now and then; it's the only way to know. The rice should be slightly firm for a salad as the dressing will break it down slightly. Cook it a little longer if you want to serve it on its own. If the rice is to be served cold, drain it in a colander and rinse well with cold water. This will stop the cooking and cool the rice quickly. If the rice is to be served hot, rinse with hot water, poke a couple of holes down to the bottom of the colander so that all the water can drain away, cover the colander with a plate and let it sit until you are ready to serve. The rice will remain hot up to 10 minutes.

### Chiffonade

Chiffonade refers to the method of cutting leafy things into thin ribbons. Lettuce, sorrel and cabbage are cut into thin shreds as a garnish for soups or a base for salads. Place one leaf upon the other in a stack, fold in half and then in quarters. Slice in tiny ribbons. When they unfold, you will discover a delicate mass of beautifully cut greens. Cut large heads of leafy vegetables in half through the core, place flat side down and shred.

## Sauté

The French verb *sauter* means "to jump." Sauté-ing is the process of cooking over very high heat in a small amount of butter or oil, searing and sealing in the juices of vegetables, meats and fish. The food should nearly jump in the pan itself; a certain amount of shaking of the pan is important so that the food really does jump, thus avoiding sticking. This works best in a sauté pan, which is a heavy pan with straight, shallow sides and a long handle. My favorite size is 5-quart.

## Blanch, Peel and Seed Tomatoes

Bring a small pan of water to a boil. Drop in a ripe tomato and wait for 30 seconds (longer if the tomato isn't quite ripe). Remove with a fork and plunge instantly into ice-cold water to stop the cooking. The tomato skin should slip easily away with only the slightest help from a paring knife. Peel the tomato while blanching the next one. Repeat until all the tomatoes are done. Cut the tomatoes in half and gently squeeze out the seeds.

The same method works splendidly with peaches; they may require slightly longer in the water—about 1 minute in all.

## Chop an Onion

To cut an onion in a tearless fashion was always a great challenge until I learned this technique. Cut off the tip end of the onion. *Do not* cut off the hairy root end. Peel. Cut the onion in half through the root and tip end, and place flat side down on the cutting surface. Keeping the root end to your left (or to the right if you are left-handed), use a sharp knife to make several horizontal cuts, parallel to the cutting board, toward the root end but not through it. Turn the onion slightly and make several parallel cuts, perpendicular to the board, and again, toward the root end but not through it. Now, holding the onion gently together with your hand, slice across all those cuts, as if you were just slicing half an onion (the root end is once more to your left). Little diced onions fall right off. As you approach the root, stop cutting—save this for your stockpot, along with the onion skins. The fineness of your dice depends on how close you slice the many parallel cuts. The closer they are together, the finer the dice; the wider they are, the larger

When you have finished, wash your hands in cold water, rubbing in a bit of salt and a squeeze of lemon.

## Mash Garlic

Cut the root end from a clove of garlic. Without peeling the clove, place the flat side of your chef's knife on the garlic and give it a sharp, fast crack with your fist or the heel of your hand. Make sure the handle of your knife hangs over the counter; it makes for a more efficient smack. Remove the knife and simply lift away the garlic peel. Place the garlic and ½ teaspoon of salt on a flat board and mash together with a small metal spatula until they form a smooth paste.

## Poach a Chicken Breast for Salad

Nothing could be easier than poaching a chicken breast, and if it is already boned the process takes no more than two or three minutes—good to remember when you are in a hurry!

If the breasts are whole, split them in two along the breastbone. Place in a single layer in a skillet, cover with hot chicken stock and a generous pinch of salt and bring to a boil. Turn down the heat and simmer just until the meat whitens and becomes firm to the touch—this may take as little as five minutes. Remove the chicken, and when it is cool enough, remove the skin and bones. Save the stock, of course!

## Roast Peppers

Roasting a pepper not only brings out its flavor, but also allows you to peel it. Many people who find fresh peppers indigestible discover that they can enjoy them once the skins have been removed.

If you have a gas stove, you can roast peppers directly over the flame on top of the stove (that's right, no pan is necessary). If your stove is electric, you will find it easier to roast them in the oven, close up under the broiler. As they blister and char, turn them over until they are "done" all around; this should take from 5 to 10 minutes.

When they have cooled, strip away the skins with your hands. Catch the juices in a plate and give your recipe an extra fillip by adding them to the oil you use.

## Cook Shrimp

This method keeps shrimp tender *and* produces a luscious stock with lots of uses. For each pound of unshelled shrimp, place two small carrots, a medium-size onion, quartered, a bay leaf, two or three peppercorns and a generous pinch salt in a pot, slightly more than cover with water and bring to a boil. Add the shrimp and cook for no more than three minutes after the water returns to the boil. Remove from the heat, cover and allow the shrimp to cool in the liquid before peeling them. Save the stock for a second batch, poaching fish, or as the beginning of a soup.

## Make a Bouquet Garni

A bouquet garni is a little bundle of tasty aromatic herbs used for flavoring savory liquids such as stocks and bouillons. A classic bouquet garni is made of parsley (the stems in particular—they are the most tasty part), thyme and a bay leaf, but there is no earthly reason why one could not include any other herb in addition to or instead of the thyme. A favorite combination of mine is to tie four or five parsley stems with a small bunch of fresh thyme, covered by a bay leaf, to a two- or three-inch piece of celery. Tie it round and round with light cotton string; I always leave a long tail so that I can tie the loose end to my stockpot handle or, in case I drop the whole thing into the pot, I always have a way to retrieve it when I'm finished.

If you are using dried herbs, they should be tied into little cheesecloth bundles (wash the cloth first in plain hot water to remove sizing or soap), or placed in mesh teaball infusers so they can be removed easily. A bouquet garni *is* usually removed so that its woody texture does not interfere with the food. It is also important to remember that herbs sometimes taste bitter if left in too long.

## Make Crème Fraîche

One of the most delightful of French ingredients is crème fraîche. It is tangy and thick and does not curdle when boiled. Many people argue that it cannot be made successfully in this country, but I for one do not agree. Making your own crème fraîche is rather like making your own yogurt. Choose sour cream that is of high quality and devoid of thickeners such as carrageenan, or use good buttermilk. Use cream with a high butterfat content, which has no added stabilizers and has not been "ultrapasteurized" or supersterilized. (The better your cream, the better your crème fraîche.)

To prepare crème fraîche, add four tablespoons of buttermilk or one pint of sour cream to a quart of good, heavy/whipping cream. Stir and heat to lukewarm. Do not exceed 85 degrees Fahrenheit or you will not induce the right bacteria to grow; you will kill them. Pour the mixture into a loosely covered jar. Place in the oven with a pilot light and leave it there overnight. If you do not have a gas oven, allow the crème fraîche to sit in a warm room for five to eight hours or in a cool room for 24 to 36 hours. Stir, cover, and refrigerate for a day to season. When you get down to the last two or three tablespoons, add another eight ounces of whipping cream and start again. This recipe goes on forever.

To substitute for crème fraîche: Use heavy cream that has been reduced by cooking it down to almost half its volume. Use sour cream if the crème fraîche is only to be used for decoration, but avoid using it as a substitute in a product that will be heated. Sour cream does not contain enough butterfat to keep it from curdling.

## Segment an Orange or Grapefruit

Cut a thin slice from the top and bottom of the fruit with a sharp knife, place base side down on a cutting board and cut off the peel in strips from the top to the bottom. Cut just deep enough to remove the bitter white pith. Move around the fruit, following its shape, until it is completely peeled. Hold it cupped in your hand so that the segments are vertical and remove each in turn from its membrane. Use a light sawing motion on either side of the membrane and work over a bowl so that you can catch the juice as well as the sections.

## Make Celery or Scallion Brushes

Wash celery ribs and cut the centers into two-inch-long sections. Score either end of each section lengthwise several times, almost to the center. Drop into a bowl of iced water and chill until the slashed ends curl back. Drain well before using.

To make a scallion brush, trim the root end from the scallion and cut a two-inch piece from the bottom. Slash this, as for the celery, through each end to the center, rotating the tiny cylinder as you go. Drop into iced water and wait—a beautiful Oriental brush will fan out.

## Prepare a Tomato Rose

Using a small sharp knife, cut a thin slice from the base of a *firm* tomato—*but do not remove it completely*. Invert the tomato so that the base is now at the top and continue cutting a thin ribbon of skin, about ¾ inch wide, around the tomato, as if you were peeling an apple in one continuous strip. If you use a gentle sawing motion, your rose will be a bit frillier, and it will be easier to cut.

Don't worry if you don't get all the way to the bottom (formerly the top) of your tomato in one piece—you will need two strips to arrange the rose. If you *have* peeled it in one piece, cut the strip in half. Wind the strip attached to the base loosely around the fleshy side of the base, forming a rose; roll the second strip up more tightly and place it in the center.

## Garnish with Cucumber Slices

Score an unpeeled cucumber from top to bottom with the tines of a fork or a lemon zester. Slice thinly and arrange in closely overlapping layers around the edge of the platter being used.

Cut thin slices from an unpeeled cucumber. Slash each slice lightly once, from edge to center, and splay it out in a twisting motion. Place firmly onto whatever requires a garnish with a little height. Tuck a parsley sprig into the spot where the cucumber twists.

For a variation, chop several tablespoons of parsley very finely and before twisting the slice, press one side firmly into the parsley. Now twist for a dual color effect.

These techniques work equally well with thin lemon or orange slices.

# Soups

# Stone Soup

Once upon a time there was a poor village in a land at war. There came into the small hamlet a company of weary soldiers. Tired and hungry, they encamped for the night near the town square. The villagers trembled, for they had no food to share with these men, and were afraid they might cause trouble. Soon the small band of men uncovered a gigantic pot and began to lay a fire for it. Trudging back and forth to the town well, they filled the pot with water and set it carefully upon the crackling fire. An old woman, peering from behind a shutter, noticed that they dropped a round stone into the pot. Unable to contain her curiosity, she ventured into the open, approached the cluster of soldiers around the pot, and after looking into the kettle, queried, "What, pray tell, are you cooking there?"

The soldiers looked up and replied, "Stone soup, my good woman, a wondrous dish and so, so much better if we were to have just a single onion or two to drop herein!" "I am but a poor peasant and have hardly enough to eat for myself," she answered, "but perhaps there is a sad onion or two on my kitchen shelf. I will bring them here for your soup if you will share a bowl of your fine repast with me." They consented, and she quietly disappeared, hungry with anticipation of the meal.

As she returned and added the onions, a querulous old man approached and after looking into the kettle, called out, "What, pray tell, are you cooking here?" "Stone soup, my good man, and a right good banquet it is," they answered, "but how much better it would be if only we had some simple carrot to add." The poor man shook his head and replied, "I am but a starving peasant, but perhaps my good wife has some carrots hidden away for our last bite of food. I would share them with you if you would share a bowl of your fine soup with me and that good woman." They nodded appreciatively and awaited the return of the old man, his old wife and the carrots. After a while, return they did, and added their meager bounty to the pot.

They all sat down and waited. A young girl with a small basket of herbs from the meadow entered the square and joined the group around the large and bubbling pot. She too was persuaded to add her share and she too waited. One by one, the hungry peasants of the village came out to see what all the excitement was about. And one by one, they added a few potatoes, a handful of beans, a small green cabbage and a bone.

There soon appeared in their midst the town butcher, who had long since closed his door. Huffing and puffing, and mopping his brow with a large red handkerchief, he called out, "What is all this commotion? What, pray tell, smells so wonderfully good here in this poor village which has nothing to eat?" "Stone soup, Sir," said the soldiers, "a creation fit for a king. All that is lacking to give it truly royal proportions is a chicken."

Oohs and aahs were heard throughout the crowd of hungry peasants. It is even said that one old woman fainted from the heavenly nature of the thought. The butcher quietly disappeared. Within a matter of minutes he returned, clutching a scrawny chicken, his very last, and dropped it, with applause from the crowd, into the pot.

There was great merriment in the town that night. It had been a long time since they had laughed and sung and danced—and a very long time since they had eaten so well. In the morning when the town awoke, the soldiers had packed up their pot and left the village, leaving behind only the stone.

They marched all day and in the evening entered another poor small town. They uncovered their gigantic pot and set about laying a fire for it. When it was successfully filled with water, they dropped in a large round stone. A nervous old man approached them and asked, "What, pray tell, are you cooking there?" "Stone soup, my good man, a wondrous dish and so, so much better if we were to have just a single onion or two to drop herein. . . ."

# On Making Stocks

As I was growing up, I heard the story of Stone Soup regularly. In a home where the cooking was always superior, soup was a wonderful event and, given that we ate it often, many wonderful events of my childhood were connected to the soup pot. Soup now, as then, connotes a sense of well-being and a sense of sharing. A pot of steaming soup banishes the blues just as quickly as a pot of chicken soup may cure the common cold. A chilled cup of cold soup refreshes a summer day. Making soup is really a relaxing experience, with considerably fewer rules than most aspects of cooking.

It seems a pity that so much mystique has grown up around the stockpot. We envision hours of labor, heavy steaming pots filled with exotic and expensive ingredients, directions far too complex to decipher and, to top it all off, nowhere to store the stuff when we've finished. How sad! A good stock is the best friend a cook can have in the kitchen; it makes a new cook a good one, and a good cook a great one. The ingredients involved are hardly exotic—in fact, they are often everyday ingredients and leftovers. The hours of time required are only those needed for the pot to sit on the stove and never does a kitchen smell better than when there's a stock under way.

So banish the mystique—making a stock is deliciously simple. And once you've learned to make one, you can make any of them successfully—only the details differ.

# Chicken Stock

*The chicken stock never stops simmering in my school and restaurant. The pot is always being added to. All manner of bits and pieces are dropped in as the week goes by and the stock turns into a soup which turns into a sauce which gets added to the soup the next week.*

*A good chicken stock begins when you tell the butcher or the man behind the supermarket counter that no, you do not want your chicken boned, you need the bones for the stock. The bones are covered with water and vegetables such as onions, leeks and carrots. A bouquet garni made up of herbs that are appropriate for the eventual use of the stock is usually added, and the stock is simmered, uncovered, for at least five hours. (To prevent any type of stock from becoming cloudy, never boil or cover it.) The stock is then strained, degreased and refrigerated.*

5 pounds chicken carcasses, wings, backs and giblets (do not use the liver, it is too bloody and will cause the stock to be cloudy)

1 large onion, stuck with 4 cloves and cut in half

3 large carrots, cut in thirds

1 leek, thinly sliced and washed carefully

4 peppercorns

Bouquet garni (see page 15)

Optional: Mushroom peelings, onion skins, tops and bottoms, and tomatoes add a depth of flavor but also darken the stock; too abundant use of celery, cabbage, cauliflower, turnips or parsnips can cause bitterness

Place the chicken bones and parts in a large pot, cover them with water and heat to boiling. Remove the scum (coagulated blood) with a slotted spoon, reduce the heat and add the vegetables, peppercorns and bouquet garni. Simmer gently, uncovered, for at least 5 hours, refilling the pot with water if it reduces down too close to the ingredients.

The cooking time can be interrupted at any time without harming the stock, but be sure to refrigerate it immediately. Chicken stock is a very rich medium for the growth of bacteria and should be cooled as quickly as possible. Do not allow it to remain at room temperature for even a little while. Refrigerate the stock, whether finished and strained or interrupted halfway, *without* a lid for rapid cooling.

When the stock has cooked long enough, strain it through a fine sieve or a piece of cheesecloth into a clean pot or bowl. Discard the cooked vegetables and bones. It is easiest to skim the fat off after the stock has chilled, as the fat will have congealed on the top. Actually, the layer of fat seals the stock and it stays fresh longer if you just push aside the fat and scoop up the stock (by now it will probably be beautifully gelatinized) with a large ladle.

When chilled, cover the stock with plastic wrap to avoid the absorption of smells. Reboil degreased refrigerated stock every 2 or 3 days to keep it bacteria-free. Season the stock with salt when you are ready to use it, as it will no longer reduce itself out of proportion. Chicken stock freezes very well.

# Brown Stock

*Makes 4-5 quarts*

*The methods for making this classic stock are similar to those used in making chicken stock. Roasting the bones and some of the vegetables in the oven prior to boiling them produces a wonderfully rich flavor.*

**6 pounds veal bones (shank bones are good), sawed in half**
**5 pounds beef shins (meat and bones), sawed in half, if necessary, to fit the pot**
**5 pounds chicken carcasses**
**8 large carrots, washed but not peeled, cut into chunks**
**2 pounds onions, cut into large chunks**
**6 cloves, stuck into the pieces of onion**
**1 whole bulb unpeeled garlic**
**4 turnips, cut in quarters**
**5 leeks, cleaned and cut in half**
**3 stalks celery, cut in quarters**
**Bouquet garni (see page 15)**
**8-10 black peppercorns**

Preheat the oven to 400 degrees. Place the bones in a large roasting pan and brown for 1 hour, turning them once. Add the onions and carrots and continue roasting for an additional 40 minutes. Transfer all the bones and vegetables to a large stockpot, using a slotted spoon. Try to leave as much fat behind in the roasting pan as possible. Cover the bones and vegetables with cold water and bring to a boil over high heat.

Discard the fat from the roasting pan and add approximately 1 cup of water to the "goodies" left in the bottom. Heat the water to boiling and scrape the pan with a wooden spoon to dissolve all the caramelized juices. Add this to the liquid in the stockpot, reduce the heat and simmer, uncovered, for 1 to 2 hours. Skim off the foam that comes to the top. Add all the remaining vegetables and the bouquet garni and simmer gently for 6 to 10 hours or more, skimming as necessary. Keep the water level well above the bones and vegetables by adding more water as required.

Strain the stock through a fine sieve into a smaller bowl or pot. Refrigerate the stock or continue cooking until the liquid has reduced and become concentrated.

# Busy Day Stock

*Although the most important ingredient in the preparation of stock is patience, a decent stock can be prepared in a hurry. By cutting all the ingredients into tiny pieces, all their flavors are released more rapidly and a good stock can be prepared in an hour and a half.*

**1 pound uncooked chicken meat, cut into small pieces**
**1 pound lean beef, cut into small pieces**
**2 carrots, finely chopped**
**1 leek, white part only, cleaned and thinly sliced**
**1 large onion, finely chopped**
**1 celery stalk, finely chopped**
**2 cloves**
**Bouquet garni (see page 15)**
**½ teaspoon salt**
**3 peppercorns**
**2 quarts water**

Place all the ingredients in a large pot, cover with cold water and slowly heat to boiling, stirring occasionally. Reduce the heat and simmer for approximately 1 hour. Carefully spoon the meat and vegetables into a cheesecloth-lined strainer and then ladle the stock through the double filter of the meat and the cloth. Skim the fat from the top of the stock with paper towels or grease mops, or use whatever method works for you.

# Vegetable Stock

*Perhaps the most difficult stock to produce is the terrifically healthy vegetable stock. Vegetable stock lacks the body and character lent by the meat and fish and bones of other broths and stocks, and requires deft handling of the vegetables balanced with just the right amount of liquid. But it is an admirable stock and can be substituted for chicken stock. Unfortunately, it does not keep well and should be used within a day.*

**2 tablespoons unsalted butter**
**4 carrots, chopped coarsely**
**1 leek, green and white parts, washed carefully and thinly sliced**
**1 onion, chopped**
**1 stalk celery with leaves, sliced**
**½ head iceberg lettuce, sliced**
**4 cups water**
**Bouquet garni (see page 15)**
**4 white peppercorns**

Heat the butter in a large skillet or stockpot. Sauté the vegetables over medium heat for 5 minutes until they are soft. Cover with cold water, add the bouquet garni and peppercorns. Bring slowly to a boil and simmer 1½ to 2 hours or until reduced to 3 cups. Strain through a fine sieve or cheesecloth and use at once or refrigerate.

# Fish Stock

**2 tablespoons butter or oil**
**1 celery stalk, chopped**
**1 large onion, sliced**
**2 carrots, sliced**
**2½ pounds fish bones and heads,**
**  rinsed**
**5-6 sprigs parsley**
**1 bay leaf**
**½-1 teaspoon salt**
**1-inch by 2-inch strip of lemon peel**
**2 quarts water**
**5-6 peppercorns**

Heat the butter in a large pan and slowly cook the vegetables and the fish bones together for 20 minutes. (The bones and heads of sweet, nonfatty fish such as red snapper, striped bass, cod, flounder, sole or whiting are best.) Do not add the skin as it is usually a bit fatty and tends to lend a grayish cast to the stock. Add the parsley, bay leaf, salt, lemon peel and water. Bring quickly to a boil, lower the heat and simmer gently for no more than 20 minutes. Add the peppercorns and simmer another 10 minutes. Strain the stock to remove the bones and vegetables, and chill.

If you wish to keep this in the refrigerator, it should be boiled every 2 or 3 days so that no bacteria can grow. Fish stock freezes well, so make some ahead; fish soups and sauces are only moments away when you have stock in your freezer.

---

## ABOUT FISH STOCKS

A FISH STOCK is made from fish trimmings and vegetables (see recipe on this page).

A COURT BOUILLON is the classic poaching liquid for fish. Combine equal quantities of dry white or red wine and water in a large nonaluminum pan. Add chopped onions, carrots, leeks and celery and bring to a boil, uncovered. Reduce the heat, add a bouquet garni and a pinch of salt. Cook for 40 minutes, adding a few peppercorns halfway through. Strain out the vegetables and return the liquid to the pot, making sure there is enough to cover the piece or pieces of fish completely. Poach the fish over very low heat for 10 minutes per inch of thickness (measured at the thickest part). To prevent the delicate fish from breaking apart, the court bouillon should never be hot enough to tremble.

A FISH FUMET is the strained, reduced essence of either fish stock or court bouillon after the fish has been poached.

# On Thickening Soups

## Reductions

A soup can be thickened simply by reducing the liquid volume by boiling or simmering. Any liquid, whether it be a stock, milk, cream, wine or water, can be reduced. Moisture evaporates in steam, the liquid gets thicker and the flavors become more intense. To reduce liquids quickly, pour them into a shallow pan with a very broad surface and boil, stirring constantly to avoid burning. To reduce more slowly, use a deeper pan and a lower flame. Soups that have raw egg, sour cream, or other ingredients that may curdle should be reduced *before* adding those ingredients. How long a reduction takes, of course, depends on the amount of liquid to be reduced and the intensity of flavor desired. Taste as you go, both for desired thickness as well as depth of flavor.

CAUTION: As a soup or sauce reduces, the herbs, and the salt in particular, seem to get stronger; there is now less liquid and a higher concentration of herbs and salt. It is better to slightly undersalt or underseason before reducing; taste for correct seasonings at the end.

## Purees

The simplest method of thickening a soup is to puree it in a food processor, or to add starchy pureed vegetables.

SEVEN STEPS IN PUREEING

1. Heat butter or oil *gently* over a low flame.
2. Cut the vegetables or meats in small or thin pieces so that they will absorb the oil or butter quickly and completely.
3. Allow the vegetables or meats to "sweat" in the butter.
4. Add a small amount of flour, *if called for.*
5. Add the liquid (vegetable, meat or fish stock, water, milk or cream), cover the soup, and simmer for 20 to 30 minutes or until the vegetables are tender, but still colorful.
6. Process the vegetables in small batches, using the steel S blade and the pulse on-and-off method. Process for a total of 30 seconds to 1 minute, adding liquid and scraping down the sides of the bowl as necessary. Repeat until all of the ingredients are processed and the puree is of the proper consistency.
7. Return the puree to the soup liquid and continue cooking.

Some vegetables do not contain sufficient starch to thicken the liquid, so you may need to add an additional vegetable puree. Mashed potatoes, rice, lima beans, winter squash and peas are frequently used to thicken soup.

## Liaisons

A liaison is added to a soup or sauce near the very end to stabilize pureed ingredients in their broth, thicken them slightly, and to add an elegant velvety finish. There are several kinds of liaison: a *roux* or *beurre manié*, a pureed rice or bread *panade*, the simple addition of arrowroot or cornstarch (*à la fécule*), and the *Allemande*, an egg yolk mixed with heavy cream. I prefer to use the last because of its finer flavor.

### ROUX

A roux is made by heating butter, gradually incorporating in it an equal amount of flour to form a smooth paste. It is often used in thickening a cream soup. It is also traditionally used for making a béchamel.

To make a simple béchamel, heat four tablespoons of butter in a saucepan, add four tablespoons flour and stir over low heat for a minute

du-
an
ing
ncy
in

' is
ded
r a
po-
hen
ken

a hot liquid by simply swishing my fork or whisk full of the beurre manié around in the hot mass.

Although you *can* add hot liquids to a hot roux, if you keep in mind the foolproof technique of using a hot roux with a cold liquid and a cold beurre manié when you have a hot liquid, your sauces, gravies and soups will never be lumpy!

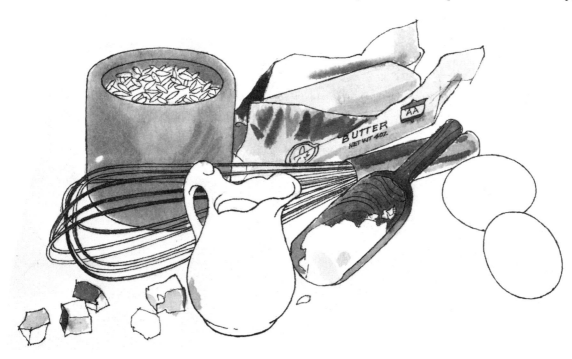

Whether you use a roux or beurre manié, remember that approximately 1 tablespoon of butter mixed with 1 tablespoon of flour will thicken 2 to 3 cups of liquid with cooking.

### PANADE

A panade is either made from scratch or with leftovers of starchy vegetables or bread, pureed to a paste and added as a thickener to soups, pâtés or mousselines. It is usually used cold and worked into the dish like a beurre manié. Stale, dry cubes of very good bread should be soaked in milk or boiling water, squeezed gently and whisked into the soup (use about ½ pound of bread to 1 cup of liquid or just put it into the soup stock and puree). Cooked rice whirled in a food processor with just enough stock to help create a paste is a panade, as is a very thick béchamel or cream puff paste without the sugar.

The equivalent of 8 thick slices of bread will be required to thicken 2 quarts of liquid.

### À LA FÉCULE

To thicken a soup à la fécule, use cornstarch, tapioca, arrowroot or potato starch. Only a small amount is required to do a lot of thickening. Dissolve 1 teaspoon of the starch in 2 tablespoons of cold water, mix, and stir into 1 pint to 1 quart of hot liquid, depending on the thickness you require. Boil *briefly* after this addition.

### ALLEMANDE

If you use any of the starch liaisons, you have the advantage of being able to bring the soup to the boil afterwards. This more delicate liaison of yolk and cream can only be gently warmed after its addition, or it will curdle. To avoid curdling the egg yolk when adding it, stir some of the hot liquid into the yolk first, warming it gently. Then add more hot liquid to it bit by bit, stirring until it is quite hot. Proceed to pour the hot yolks back into the hot soup or sauce with moderate abandonment, now they are no longer shocked by the heat. It takes 2 egg yolks to thicken about 1 cup of liquid.

NOTE: If any amount of starch or flour is present in a soup with an egg and cream liaison, it will have sufficient binding power to prevent curdling even when the soup is returned to the boiling point.

## SOUPS BASED ON MEAT AND FISH

# Chicken Soup

*Serves 6*

*Rich in memories of childhood, joy of the Jewish mother, nothing tastes as wonderful as a steaming bowl of rich golden chicken soup with matzo balls. Noodles or rice would be nice, too. Try adding the little liver dumplings in the next recipe to this fine soup.*

**3-pound chicken, or a hen if possible (include gizzards, hearts, wings and backs, but not the livers)**
**2 medium-size onions, each studded with 3 cloves and cut in half**
**Handful of parsley**
**2 parsnips, sliced**
**1 large sprig fresh dill, or up to 1 teaspoon dry**
**3 medium-size carrots (peeled only if you plan to serve them with the soup), sliced**
**2 stalks celery with leaves, sliced**
**10 peppercorns**
**1 teaspoon salt**

Put the chicken and the giblets in a large pot; cover with cold water. Heat to boiling and pour off all the water. Rinse the chicken quickly to remove all the coagulated blood. Wash the pot. This technique ensures a crystal-clear soup.

Cover the chicken again with cold water and cook over medium heat for about 25 minutes. Do not cover the pot with a lid and do not let the soup boil. Add the vegetables and peppercorns and cook for another 20 to 30 minutes. Add the dill and salt to taste and cook for at least another half hour. Strain the soup, skim off the fat, adjust the seasoning and serve at once. Or, better yet, allow to cool in the refrigerator overnight (don't cover until cold; the lid just delays the cooling). When the soup is cool, skim off the solid fat. The chicken from a chicken soup usually has little taste left at this point so I don't usually bother to save it.

# Chicken Liver Dumplings

*Serves 8*

*When our children were small and I was designing toys for Fisher-Price, we had a German nanny who came in to watch the children. At age 70, when she wasn't reading to them, teaching them to cha-cha, or cleaning, she was cooking up a storm. This was Nanna's recipe.*

**1 pound beef, calf or chicken liver**
**1 small onion, finely chopped**
**1 raw egg**
**Grated rind of 1 lemon**
**Salt to taste**
**2 scallions, green part only, finely chopped**

Combine the liver, onion, egg, lemon and salt in the food processor. Stir in the scallion greens by hand. Press the mixture through a spaetzle maker with very large holes or through a flat open grater into lightly salted boiling water. Poach the dumplings for about 3 minutes or just until firm. Serve in a clear soup.

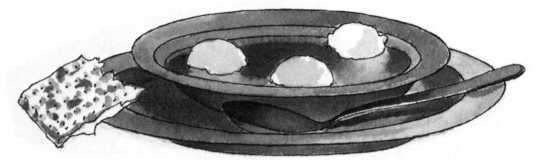

# Perfect Matzo Balls

*Makes 12 balls*

*There is one school of opinion that adores hard, chewy matzo balls and another that sings praises to the light and fluffy variety. For years, I have made both kinds, just in case.*

**1 cup matzo meal**
**½ teaspoon salt**
**3 eggs, well beaten**
**3 tablespoons chicken fat, melted**
**½ cup water**

Blend the matzo meal with the salt, eggs and chicken fat. Add sufficient water to bind the ingredients together. Refrigerate for at least 1 hour.

Wet your hands and form the mixture into small balls; they will expand enormously. Bring a large quantity of salted water to a boil and reduce the heat to just below the boiling point. Slip the matzo balls, a few at a time, into the simmering water and cook gently for 15 minutes. Do not crowd the pan. When the balls rise to the top of the water, they will be fully cooked.

NOTE: I do not recommend cooking the matzo balls directly in the traditional chicken soup. Any balls that fall apart during cooking will turn your soup into a disaster.

# "EMBROIDERY" FOR CHICKEN SOUP

*The classic French cookbooks, Escoffier in particular, list literally hundreds of elegant garnishes for soup. Here are a few that are easy to execute and delicious to eat.*

## CHICKEN NOODLE SOUP

Chicken soup is never more warmly familiar than when served with a handful of precooked pasta per person. For a delightful change, try the little stars made of pasta or *riso*, which is pasta shaped like grains of rice.

## SIMPLE EGG-DROP SOUP

For each 2 servings of soup, beat an egg and pour it into the soup in a thin stream, from a fairly high distance, stirring all the time.

## CHICKEN CONSOMMÉ CELESTINE

Try thinly shredded, cold leftover crêpes or tiny empty cream puffs for a typical French finish to a chicken consommé.

## CHICKEN CONSOMMÉ FLAVIGNY

Sauté 10 (if you're lucky) fresh morels in enough butter so that the morels have no chance of sticking. Add a couple of tablespoons of cooked rice and a tablespoon of julienned, cooked chicken breast. Makes enough garnish for 8 or 9 cups of soup.

## CHICKEN CONSOMMÉ BRUNOISE

Dice 3 medium-size carrots, 1 turnip, half an onion and 2 ribs of celery into ⅛-inch cubes. Sauté the dice in 4 tablespoons of butter with a pinch of salt. When the carrots are just barely tender, add a cup or two of stock. When ready to serve, add the rest of the stock and a couple of tablespoons of tiny peas.

# A Clarified Consommé

*There is no soup as exquisite as a crystal-clear, perfectly flavored consommé. Served hot or jellied, it is a thing of rare beauty and a true test of a cook's skill.*

2 quarts well-seasoned cold rich beef, chicken or fish stock

¾ pound lean beef, ground or minced finely, or shredded fish if using fish stock

½ cup dry sherry, dry Madeira, or white wine, if using fish stock

¾ cup tomatoes, peeled, seeded and diced (see page 14)

2 carrots, minced

1 leek, white and green parts, cleaned and minced

½ teaspoon ground black pepper

3 egg whites, slightly beaten

2 eggshells, crushed

Salt to taste

Garnish with lemon wedges or paper-thin slices of raw mushroom

Pour the stock into a large stainless steel or enamel saucepan and add the meat, wine and vegetables. Add the beaten egg whites and crushed eggshells. Bring to a boil over medium heat, whisking steadily. Stop stirring and simmer gently for 1 hour. Do not allow the liquid to boil and do not disturb the "crust" that forms on the surface. Gently spoon the foam and crust onto a cheesecloth-lined strainer and carefully ladle the consommé through the double filter. Taste, and add more salt if necessary. Chill the consommé.

Serve cold, garnished with small lemon wedges or serve hot with paper-thin mushroom slices.

# French Onion Soup

*Onion soup, for all its mystique, is one of the simplest of soups to make. Its success lies in the quality of the ingredients. Because there's really very little in it, make sure that you use the very best of everything: never canned stock, cubes or granules. Once it's assembled, just close your eyes, take a deep breath and you'll be transported straight to the markets of Paris.*

**2 tablespoons olive oil**
**3 tablespoons unsalted butter**
**6 cups thinly sliced yellow onions**
**½ teaspoon sugar**
**½ teaspoon salt**
**4 tablespoons all-purpose flour**
**2½ quarts hot strong brown stock,**
  **very rich chicken stock, or**
  **vegetable stock**
**¾ cup dry white wine**
**Salt and pepper to taste**
**8 slices slightly stale French bread**
**2 cups thinly sliced or grated**
  **Jarlsberg or Gruyère cheese**
**¼ cup brandy**

Heat the oil in a heavy skillet. Add the butter. When the butter has melted, add the onions and cook slowly, covered, for 10 minutes. Add the salt. Raise the heat, remove the lid, add the sugar and stir the onions until golden. If you want a deeper flavor, allow the onions to caramelize slightly and turn a rich dark brown color; do not let them burn! This process should take at least half an hour. Sprinkle flour over the onions; stir and cook until a paste has formed. This creates a roux. Remove from the heat, stir in the hot stock and wine, and season to taste. Simmer, uncovered, for 30 minutes. Skim off any visible oil from the surface of the soup.

Toast the slices of French bread until crisp and lightly browned. Pour the soup into a soup tureen or an ovenproof casserole. Float the toasted bread on top of the soup and cover with the cheese. Bake at 350 degrees for about 20 minutes or brown under a hot broiler for 5 minutes until the cheese is bubbling. Break the cheese crust slightly and stir in the brandy. Serve immediately.

NOTE: If you wish to present this soup in individual bowls, set them on a heavy cookie sheet when you put them in the oven or under the broiler. This makes the hot bowls easier to handle.

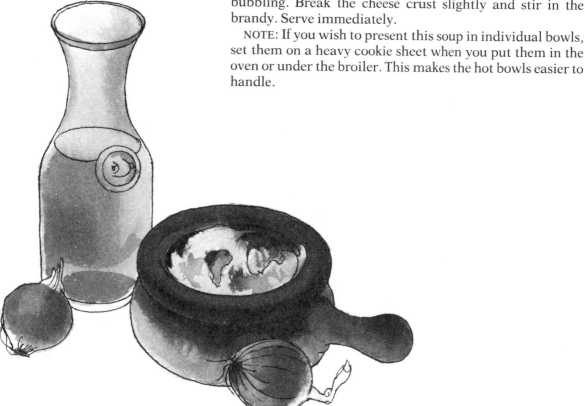

# Sicilian Fish Soup

*Although I grew up in New England, spent time on the southern coast of France, and cooked in the kitchens of Taipei, never have I seen such an abundance of beautiful seafood as in Sicily. Markets in Palermo and the old part of Syracuse are filled with small red mullets, squid and octopus of every size and color, fresh tuna and swordfish. They are displayed boldly and artfully: all facing in the same direction, glistening with freshness. The new catch is arranged twice a day, once for the midday meal and once for the evening meal. In Sicily, with endless varieties of tomatoes and peppers, fish soup is heaven.*

¼ cup virgin green Italian or French olive oil (first pressing)

4 medium-size carrots, finely chopped

2 large onions, diced

2 leeks, white part only, washed carefully and diced

3-6 garlic cloves depending on your taste (do not remove the peel)

2 stalks celery with leaves, diced

1 handful parsley including the stems, chopped

1 large pinch saffron

½ cup fresh fennel tops, chopped, or 2 tablespoons dried fennel

2 2-inch-by-1-inch strips each of orange peel and lemon peel, white part removed

1 large pinch dry oregano

4 cups Italian plum tomatoes, if fresh, blanched, peeled and seeded (see page 14); if canned, drained (reserve liquid)

3 tablespoons tomato paste, if necessary

1 cup water or tomato liquid

1 cup dry white wine

6 cups fish stock (see page 23)

1-2 long, red, hot peppers, fresh if possible, chopped finely

Salt and pepper to taste

Heat the olive oil in a large 5- or 6-quart pan that has a tight-fitting lid. Add the carrots, onions and leeks. Cook for 5 minutes until the onions are transparent but not limp. Add the unpeeled garlic (the skin keeps the garlic very sweet while it stews), the celery and the parsley stems. Sauté all together until you begin to smell the garlic. Add the parsley, saffron and fennel. Stir to combine and sauté briefly. Add all the remaining ingredients except the vinegar and the fish, cover, and allow to simmer for 30 minutes. If the soup does not seem rich enough at this time, add the tomato paste. This recipe can be prepared in advance up to this point.

Small fish should be cut into 1-inch steaks, while large fish should be cut into 1½-inch pieces; they do not have to be uniformly sized, in fact irregular pieces are better than even cubes. Salt the fish lightly. Add the vinegar to the soup and taste to correct the seasonings. Nestle the tougher fish just into the top of the soup. Baste well with the liquids and cook over medium heat for about 5 minutes. Add the other fish in the same manner, tucking them among the tomatoes. Simmer for 30 minutes, or until the fish is cooked through.

Transfer the fish to a preheated soup tureen and keep warm. Bring the liquid to a boil, taste one last time and ladle carefully over the fish. Pass the toasted bread and cheese.

NOTE: It is customary throughout Europe to cook the fish heads and bones in the soup. In America it is more popular to prepare a well-seasoned fish fumet (see page 00) in advance and use this as the base of the soup.

This soup can also be found elsewhere in Sicily, around Trapani and Erice, cooked down to a thick stew and served over couscous. It is also served as a pasta course over very thick spaghetti noodles called *bucatini*.

**3-4 pounds fish** (fresh tuna, swordfish, red snapper, red mullet, haddock, cod, sea bass or monkfish, or any combination of fish you like)
**2 tablespoons white wine vinegar**
**Garnish: 16 slices French bread,** browned in the oven; freshly grated Parmesan, preferably Parmigiano Reggiano

## New England Clam Chowder

*Serves 6-8*

*There is nothing particularly unusual about this recipe; it's a perfect chowder, that's all. I learned to make it one summer when visiting friends in Woods Hole, Massachusetts. "Dig your own Quahogs," the old fisherman had begun. However, we found the prospect daunting and bought ours; you can do the same, or substitute a pound of cod for the clams and make Fish Chowder. If you cut the cod into small pieces, it will flake as it is cooked through.*

**¼ pound bacon, diced**
**2 tablespoons oil**
**4 potatoes, peeled and diced**
**1½ cups finely chopped onion**
**2 large cloves garlic**
**2 cups light cream or 2 cups evaporated milk**
**2 cups milk**
**Salt and lots of pepper**
**2 cups minced clams and as much of their juices as you can retrieve**
**2-3 tablespoons unsalted butter**
**Freshly ground black pepper**

Sauté the diced bacon in oil until the fat begins to render. Add the diced potatoes and cook for 5 minutes, tossing now and then to prevent sticking. Add the onions and garlic and cook for 5 minutes until they are transparent. Cover the pot and cook another 10 minutes until the potatoes are barely tender. Add the cream and milk, salt and pepper and simmer for 15 to 20 minutes. Add the clams and their juices or the fish, if used; heat through and taste for flavorings. Serve with a little butter melting on the top and a generous grinding of fresh black pepper.

# Pea or Lentil Soup with Ham

*Either of these soups is wonderful served with a piece of robust Polish sausage (precooked before being added to the soup) and a chunk of peasant French bread. For a more genteel approach you can garnish the soup with butter-fried croutons (see page 68).*

**16 ounces dried peas or lentils**
**1½ quarts cold water**
**2 teaspoons salt**
**1 large onion studded with 4 whole cloves**
**2 carrots cut in quarters**
**Bouquet garni (see page 15)**
**1 ham bone with some meat on it**
**½ teaspoon chervil or tarragon, if using peas, or ½ teaspoon cumin, if using lentils**
**Salt and pepper to taste**
**1 tablespoon brown sugar**
**4 tablespoons unsalted butter**
**¼ cup sherry**
**Garnish (optional): ½ cup butter-fried croutons**

If you are using dried peas, soak them overnight in cold water to cover. Remove any pieces that float to the top, and then drain. If you are using lentils, rinse and pick them over for bad ones. Add the peas or lentils to the cold water and bring to a boil. Skim the foam. Add salt and all the remaining ingredients except the brown sugar, butter and sherry. Turn down the heat and allow the soup to simmer, uncovered, until the peas or lentils are soft (about 1½ hours).

Strain the soup and reserve the liquid. Remove the bouquet garni and the ham bone from the vegetables. Pick the cloves out of the onion. Puree the vegetables in a food processor with the steel S blade, in a food mill or a blender, and return the puree to the pot. Pour the reserved liquid back in. Cut away pieces of ham remaining from the bone and add them to the soup as well. Simmer for 10 to 15 minutes. Taste for seasonings. Just before serving, stir in the sugar, butter and sherry.

# Turkey Rice Soup

*Turkey is truly a wondrous food. It smells heavenly when first roasting, it makes mouth-watering sandwiches with Russian dressing or hot gravy, and finally, after transformations into casseroles and tetrazzini, even the carcass provides a meal.*

**1 turkey carcass with some meat
   still on it**
**Water to cover**
**2 onions, quartered**
**1 bay leaf**
**4 carrots, quartered**
**4 cloves garlic**
**Salt and pepper to taste**
**1 cup uncooked rice**
**2 cups dry red wine**
**3 tablespoons brandy**
**Leftover gravy, if any**
**1 teaspoon dry thyme**

Cut away the larger pieces of turkey meat that cling to the bones and reserve. Disjoint the thigh or leg bones and the wings, if still attached. Break the body of the carcass in half or thirds. Place all the bones in a large (12-quart) stockpot and cover with water. Add the onions, bay leaf, carrots and garlic. Bring to a boil, uncovered, and skim when necessary. Simmer for 2 to 3 hours, adding water as needed to keep the bones just covered.

Strain the soup through a fine sieve. Discard the bones, onions and the bay leaf, but reserve the carrots. Add the rice and cook for 15 minutes. Add the wine and salt and pepper to taste. Cook at least another 15 minutes or until the rice is done. Add the brandy, the gravy, if any, thyme, reserved turkey pieces and carrots, and cook just long enough to heat the meat through. Adjust seasonings and enjoy with crunchy French bread.

# Steve's Scotch Broth

*Our family loves leg of lamb. We trim it of all but a very thin layer of fat, stud it with slivers of garlic and roast it until the meat is just pink. When we have finished with it, we make soup. The more meat left on the bone, the better the soup.*

**1 roasted leg of lamb, with some
   meat still on the bone**
**2-3 quarts water, to cover the bone**
**Chopped carrots, onions and celery,
   3 cups total**
**2 bay leaves**
**1 teaspoon dry thyme**
**½ cup barley**
**Salt and pepper to taste**

Put the lamb in a large stockpot, cover with the water, bring to a boil, and reduce the heat to a simmer. Simmer, uncovered, 1 to 2 hours, until the meat falls easily from the bone. Reserve the meat and cut in chunks. At this point, the lamb stock can be set aside to cool; if placed in the refrigerator the fat can be easily removed once it has congealed.

To proceed, add the vegetables, bay leaves, thyme and barley to the stock. Cook 1 to 2 hours more, or until the barley is tender. Skim off any fat that rises to the top. Add salt and pepper to taste. Serve with the chunks of tender meat.

# Old-Fashioned Vegetable Soup

*Serves 8*

*Vegetable soup is a wonderful way to use up what's in your refrigerator. Small amounts of fresh vegetables, too few to serve alone, make a miracle in a pot, when served together as soup. Use vegetable, chicken or brown stock, depending on what you have or what you want. Add pasta, meat or poultry and you quickly have a meal in a bowl.*

**7 cups stock**
**4-5 cups diced vegetables (carrots, potatoes, green beans, lima beans, broccoli and cauliflower, for example)**
**4 tablespoons butter**
**½ teaspoon dried herbs (basil, thyme or crushed rosemary)**
**Salt and pepper to taste**

Bring the stock to a boil. Sauté each vegetable separately in a small amount of the butter, until they are just barely tender. Add the vegetables, herbs and salt and pepper to the hot stock. Simmer for 20 to 30 minutes. Serve steaming hot.

# Italian Minestrone

*Serves 8 as a first course, 4 as a main course*

1 cup onions, coarsely chopped
2 large garlic cloves, minced
4 tablespoons olive oil
¼ pound kidney beans, soaked
   overnight
8 cups rich stock, preferably brown
   stock
2 tablespoons tomato paste
4 cups mixed fresh vegetables
   (cabbage, string beans and
   zucchini)
3 ripe tomatoes, blanched, peeled,
   seeded and chopped (see page 14),
   or use the equivalent of canned
   tomatoes, drained and chopped
Salt and pepper to taste
½ teaspoon dried basil
½ teaspoon dried oregano
1 cup broken vermicelli
⅓ cup freshly grated Parmesan
   (preferably Parmigiano
   Reggiano)

Sauté the onions and garlic in olive oil for 5 minutes. When the onions have just begun to take on color, add the beans and the stock and simmer, covered, for 1 hour. Dissolve the tomato paste in 1 cup of the hot stock and add to the pot along with the cabbage and tomatoes. Add salt and pepper and herbs to taste; simmer for 15 minutes. Add the remaining vegetables and the vermicelli and simmer another 15 minutes, or until the pasta is cooked. Taste and adjust the seasoning. Serve sprinkled thickly with Parmesan.

# Provençal Basil Soup (Pistou)

*Serves 8 as a first course, 4 as a main course*

*Although originally from Genoa, this Italian vegetable soup is most popular in the south of France.*

**8 cups rich stock**
**Salt and pepper to taste**
**2 pounds fresh green beans or**
   **2 pounds mixed green and yellow,**
   **tips removed and sliced on the**
   **diagonal into 1-inch pieces**
**3 large potatoes, peeled and cubed**
   **into ½-inch cubes**
**2 large ripe tomatoes, blanched,**
   **peeled, seeded and chopped (see**
   **page 14), or use the equivalent of**
   **canned tomatoes, drained and**
   **chopped**
**½ pound broken vermicelli**

**PISTOU:**
**3 large garlic cloves**
**¼ cup packed fresh basil leaves**
   **(there is no substitute)**
**4 tablespoons fruity olive oil**
**¼ cup finely grated Gruyère cheese**

Bring the stock to a boil, add the vegetables, salt and pepper to taste, and cook over medium heat for 20 minutes. The soup can be made ahead to this point and reheated while you prepare the pistou. Chop the garlic in the food processor in short on-and-off pulses. Add the basil leaves and chop finely. Remove the pusher from the feed-tube opening and dribble in the oil in a thin stream. Add the vermicelli to the soup and cook for 15 minutes.

Dilute the pistou with 4 tablespoons of hot soup and pour into a large soup tureen. Add finely grated Gruyère and ladle in the soup, stirring continuously.

NOTE: I have eaten this soup with red kidney beans added to the pot, which suggests that you may substitute the minestrone recipe. Add the pistou as above.

# French Country Garbure
*Serves 8 as a first course, 4 as a main course*

*A country soup popular throughout France, garbure is served with a "croûte au fromage" (a crunchy slice of toasted French bread covered with melted cheese). Any of the preceding recipes for vegetable soup can be served this way. I recommend using only fresh vegetables for this soup and changing them with the season.*

| IN WINTER USE: | IN SPRING USE: | IN SUMMER USE: | IN FALL USE: |
|---|---|---|---|
| 3 medium-size potatoes, peeled | 3 medium-size potatoes, peeled | 3 medium-size potatoes, peeled | 3 medium-size potatoes, peeled |
| 3 large carrots, peeled | 4 ounces celery root, peeled | 1 cup string beans or peas | 5 ounces fresh pumpkin |
| 3 turnips, peeled | 3 leeks, whites only | 3 leeks, whites only | 3 medium-size onions |

2 cups stock or water
Salt and pepper to taste
3 medium-size cloves garlic
½ teaspoon dried thyme or
  1 teaspoon fresh
1½ cups cabbage chiffonade (see
  page 13)
1 cup cooked starchy beans (chick
  peas, kidney beans, Great
  Northern beans, etc.)
1½ cups tomato puree, fresh, if
  possible
2 tablespoons minced fresh parsley

CROÛTE AU FROMAGE:
6 slices French bread cut medium
  thick and dried on a cake rack in
  the oven (do not allow to burn)
2 tablespoons unsalted butter
1 cup grated Gruyère or Jarlsberg
  cheese
Chopped parsley

Slice the root vegetables very thin; use the peas or beans whole. Slice the onions ¼ inch thick and cut the pumpkin into 1-inch cubes. Add the appropriate vegetables to the stock. Season with salt and pepper to taste and add the garlic and the thyme. Cover, and cook over low heat for 15 to 20 minutes, until the vegetables are tender. Add the cabbage and cook for 15 minutes more.

Meanwhile, puree the beans in a food processor, blender or in a food mill. Mix with a little hot stock to thin as necessary. Stir the pureed beans into the soup. Add the tomato puree. You may now puree the entire soup if you wish; I prefer to puree only part of it and enjoy the pieces. Either way, puree enough to create a very thick soup. Adjust the seasonings.

Butter the dried bread slices, spread cheese over each slice and broil in the oven until the cheese melts. Place the croûtes in the bottom of the bowl or tureen before ladling in the soup, or float them on the soup's surface. Sprinkle on the parsley and serve.

In the United States it is said that an apple a day keeps the doctor away. In France a concerned Frenchman pours a glass of red or white wine into the bottom of his bowl (after eating his vegetables, of course), mixes it with any soup that's left and drinks it down. This serves for him as the apple does for us.

# Senegalese Carrot Soup

*This soup is served in my restaurant, where the recipe is requested over and over again. It was "created" when the kitchen team was headed up by a talented young woman named Nancy. For those people who have asked and asked for this recipe, here it is at last!*

**1 small onion, finely chopped**
**3 cups medium-size carrots, peeled and coarsely chopped**
**4-6 tablespoons unsalted butter**
**3 cups hot rich chicken or vegetable stock**
**1½ cups rich milk or cream**
**2 teaspoons curry powder**
**Salt and pepper to taste**
**Garnish: Crème fraîche (see page 15) or whipped cream; 1 teaspoon ground coriander; fresh parsley**

Heat 4 tablespoons butter in a large skillet. Sauté the onions for 5 minutes until transparent, then add the carrots. Cook until the carrots are tender, adding more butter if necessary. Add the hot stock to the pan and bring to a boil. Puree in a food processor or pass the soup through a food mill. If you want a really velvety texture, push the puree through a fine sieve. Whisk in the milk or cream. Add the curry, salt and pepper to taste. Return the soup to the pan and simmer until heated through. Adjust the seasonings. Pour into hot individual soup bowls (this looks particularly pretty in white porcelain) and garnish with crème fraîche or whipped cream flavored with coriander. A single leaf of parsley on each dollop of cream is very attractive.

For a slightly different presentation, spread a thin layer of heavy cream across the top of the soup in each bowl. Place under the broiler just long enough to take on color. Serve piping hot!

NOTE: This soup can be made ahead and reheated or served cold. It is also a particularly good soup to make using Busy Day stock as the base (see page 22).

# Gazpacho (Cold Spanish Vegetable Salad Soup)

*Serves 6*

*Gazpacho is a cool beginning for a summer dinner, and a favorite of my family's for supper on a humid Midwestern evening. Always keep a supply in your refrigerator; it's an instant refresher!*

1 clove garlic
4 large ripe tomatoes, blanched, peeled, seeded and diced (see page 14)
½ sweet red pepper, diced
½ sweet green pepper, diced
1 cucumber, peeled, seeded and diced
3 scallions, chopped (whites as well as greens)
½ purple onion, diced
¼ cup finely chopped fresh parsley
1½ teaspoons chopped fresh basil
1½ teaspoons chopped fresh dill
⅓ cup light, fruity olive oil
3 tablespoons lemon or lime juice
2½ cups very light chicken stock (may be half tomato juice)
Ice cubes

Rub a large clear glass bowl with the cut side of the garlic. Combine all the chopped vegetables and stir to mix. (If you wish to use the food processor to chop your vegetables, process a small amount of each vegetable at a time, removing them before they get too mushy.) Sprinkle the vegetables with the parsley and herbs. Combine the olive oil with the lemon or lime juice and slowly dribble the mixture over the vegetables. Stir the stock into the aromatic mass and refrigerate for at least 2 hours. Serve icy cold with a few ice cubes in the bowl.

NOTE: I like my gazpacho crunchy, but if you find this soup too "textured," you may puree part of it, combine it with the remainder, and only have half the amount of chopped vegetables to deal with.

# Elegant Seafood Gazpacho

*Serves 6*

½ pound fresh scallops

MARINADE:
¾ cup freshly squeezed lime juice
1 tablespoon light olive oil
Generous pinch salt
1 teaspoon red pepper flakes
¼ teaspoon ground coriander

Trim the scallops; if they are large, cut them in smaller pieces. Combine the marinade ingredients in a small bowl. Add the scallops and marinate for 24 hours. When the fish has been cured, add it to the gazpacho mixture.

# Spicy Tomato Soup

*Although you may have the urge to break up crackers in this soup, don't do it! This is a sophisticated treat and we thank the Woodbine Cottage, a New Hampshire restaurant known for its inspiring dishes, for introducing it to us.*

**SOUP:**

**10 pounds fresh, juicy red tomatoes, blanched, peeled and seeded (see page 14)**

**3 stalks celery with leaves**

**1 small onion stuck with 7 whole cloves**

**2 bay leaves, broken in half**

**1 small bunch parsley**

**BEURRE MANIÉ**

**5 tablespoons unsalted butter at room temperature**

**5 tablespoons flour**

**½-1 tablespoon salt, according to taste**

**3 tablespoons sugar**

**½ teaspoon ground cloves**

**⅛ teaspoon cinnamon**

**GARNISH:**

**⅓ cup heavy cream, whipped with a pinch of salt**

**2 tablespoons finely chopped fresh basil leaves**

Bring all the soup ingredients to a boil and simmer for 2 hours. Remove the celery, onion, cloves, bay leaves and parsley. Puree and then strain the tomatoes. (I have made this soup ahead to this point and have even canned it for use throughout the winter.)

Blend the beurre manié ingredients together. Add 2 cups of the hot tomato puree to the beurre manié; whisk until smooth. Add this thickened mixture to the remaining puree and heat through. Serve in hot bowls garnished with a spoonful of cold whipped cream and chopped basil.

NOTE: This soup is also delicious served cold with a paper-thin slice of orange afloat in it.

# Beet Borscht

*I never tire of teaching this wonderful recipe or of eating the result. The color is exquisite and the taste is delectable. Surprisingly, even people who don't usually like beets always seem to like this.*

**2 pounds fresh untrimmed beets, or the equivalent of canned, small beets, drained**
**1½ cups beet liquid (add water to canned, if necessary)**
**3½ cups buttermilk**
**½ cup sour cream**
**2 hard-cooked eggs, chopped**
**1 cucumber, peeled, seeded and diced**
**¼ teaspoon sugar**
**6 tablespoons minced scallion greens**
**1 tablespoon dried dill, or 2½ tablespoons fresh**
**1 hot boiled potato per person (optional)**

To cook the fresh beets, wash but do not peel them. Leave about an inch of the stems attached to the beet, as well as the little root. Drop into salted boiling water to cover and boil with the lid on for 35 to 45 minutes, or until the beets are tender. Remove the beets to a plate and allow to cool. Reserve the liquid.

Peel the beets carefully, removing stems and roots, and grate them coarsely with a hand grater or in the food processor. Mix with the beet juice and chill. Stir in the buttermilk and the sour cream. Remove at least half of the beets and a good portion of the liquid, with a lot of sour cream, to the bowl of the food processor, fitted with a steel S blade. Puree. Return the puree to the rest of the soup and add the eggs, cucumbers and sugar. Sprinkle with scallions and dill to garnish. It is traditional but not essential to eat cold beet borscht with a hot boiled potato in it.

# Vichyssoise

*Served hot, this soup is warm and comforting to the soul and to the body. Served cold, it is sophisticated and refreshing. Try it both ways.*

**4 leeks, well cleaned and trimmed**
**1 celery heart**
**4 medium-size onions, peeled**
**2 pounds potatoes, peeled**
**4 tablespoons butter**
**6 cups rich stock**
**3 teaspoons salt**
**1 quart light cream or use half milk and half cream**
**2 egg yolks**
**4 tablespoons chopped chives**

Dice all the vegetables into half-inch cubes. Sauté in butter until they are barely tender, but without color. Add enough stock to cover the vegetables by at least 1 inch. Add salt. Bring to a boil, turn down the heat and allow to cook gently for no more than 30 minutes until the potatoes are cooked through. Puree the soup in a food mill or food processor. Return the puree to the stockpot and stir in half the cream. Mix the remainder of the cream with the egg yolks, and add a few tablespoons of the hot soup. Pour the cream mixture back into the soup and stir to combine. Do not boil after the addition of the cream and eggs. Taste for salt and pepper. Serve steaming hot with a sprinkling of chives.

To serve cold, simply cool without a cover, then chill for several hours.

# New Orleans Cream of Lettuce Soup

*Serves 8-10*

*A favorite New Orleans lenten dish, this soup is created in a somewhat unusual manner by making a roux on top of vegetables and then adding stock. Any combination of vegetables can be treated in this way to make a handsome cream of vegetable soup.*

4 heads Boston lettuce or equivalent
   weight of other lettuce
6 tablespoons unsalted butter
1 cup chopped shallots, whites of
   scallions, or yellow onions
1 cup chopped fresh spinach leaves
   (optional for color)
Large pinch sugar
¼ cup flour
6 cups chicken or vegetable stock
Salt and pepper to taste
¼ teaspoon grated nutmeg
2 teaspoons fresh chervil or
   1 teaspoon dried
1 teaspoon sherry pepper or
   ½ teaspoon Tabasco sauce
1 egg yolk
1 cup heavy cream
Garnish: Crème fraîche (see page
   15) or sour cream; salted
   Macadamia nuts, chopped

Chiffonade the lettuce (see page 13). Heat the butter in a large skillet and cook the shallots for 5 minutes until they have softened. Add the lettuce, cover the pan, and steam for 3 minutes until it has wilted. Add the spinach and sugar and sauté until the lettuce begins to take on a brighter color. Stir in the flour and cook for 1 or 2 minutes until it has lost its raw taste. Stir in 6 cups of the stock. Cover and simmer, stirring occasionally, for 10 minutes. Add the salt and pepper, nutmeg, chervil and sherry pepper. Add more stock if the soup becomes too thick. Adjust the lid so the pan is partially covered and simmer for another 20 minutes.

Puree the soup in a food processor. Stir the egg yolk and cream in the bottom of a warm soup tureen to make a liaison (see page 25). Stir a cup of the hot soup into the egg mixture (if you don't do this, you may scramble your egg). Add the remaining hot soup.

Float a fair-sized dollop of crème fraîche in the center of the soup and sprinkle with the chopped nuts.

# Zucchini and Cheddar Soup

*Serves 6-8*

*When the season is bountiful, everyone I know is rushing about trying to give away zucchini in the name of kindness (we all know it's really insanity). Here is my donation to the myriad recipes (from chocolate cake to pickles) that glorify this prolific vegetable.*

2 cups finely chopped onions
3 tablespoons unsalted butter
12 small zucchini, cut into julienne
    or coarsely grated
1 teaspoon dried rosemary, crushed
    with a mortar and pestle
3 cups hot chicken or vegetable
    stock
1 teaspoon salt
½ teaspoon pepper
1 teaspoon sugar
1 cup light cream
2 cups grated cheddar cheese
Fresh chives, chopped

Sauté the onions in butter until pale golden. Add the julienned zucchini and the rosemary and toss them in the butter until sizzling. Do not let the zucchini get completely soft. Turn off the heat and remove half to two thirds of the vegetables to a food processor or food mill. Puree them. Return the puree to the pan with the remaining julienned vegetables and add the hot chicken stock, salt, pepper and sugar. Heat just to boiling, then turn down the heat and stir in the cream. Do not allow the soup to boil after the cream has been added or it may curdle.

Distribute the cheese evenly among the individual soup bowls and ladle the soup on top. Garnish with chives placed carefully in the center of each bowl.

NOTE: It is important to use a good cheddar in this recipe.

# Cream of Broccoli Soup

*Serves 6-8*

2 medium-size heads (about
    1½ pounds each) fresh broccoli,
    washed, or 3 10-ounce packages
    frozen broccoli
4-6 tablespoons unsalted butter
1 onion, chopped
2 cups béchamel sauce (see page 25)
2 cups chicken or vegetable stock
Milk or stock for thinning
Salt and pepper
Pinch mace
8 pecans, lightly sautéed in
    3 tablespoons butter and
    1 teaspoon chopped garlic

Have ready a large pot of boiling salted water. Trim an inch off the broccoli stalks. Cut away the florets with an inch or two of stem, break into small units and reserve. Peel the larger stalks, quarter them and cook for 8 minutes. Add the florets, and cook for 2 minutes, uncovered. Drain the vegetables and rinse immediately with plenty of cold water. Cut the stalks into small pieces.

Heat 4 tablespoons of butter in the bottom of the pot and cook the onions until soft. Add the broccoli stalks and continue cooking. Add three-quarters of the florets and toss, adding more butter if necessary. Add the béchamel and stir, adding the stock to blend well. Remove the vegetables with a slotted spoon and puree them in the food processor with the steel S blade, using short on-and-off pulses.

Return the pureed soup to a clean pot, add seasonings and simmer for 30 minutes. Thin, if necessary, with milk or stock. Garnish with the remaining florets and pecans.

# Hot and Sour Soup (Swan La Tang) – For Eric

*My husband and I teach Chinese cooking together and every time we schedule a class that includes this soup we have to put it on the calendar twice to accommodate everyone who wants to learn how to make it. Many ingredients given here have a choice of amounts; that is because the quantities of the ingredients can be varied to suit your own taste. If your budget permits, and if you like your soup hearty, add the larger choice of ingredients. If you like it hotter, add all the pepper; if sourer, add more vinegar. If you prefer it soupier, use the smaller amount of vegetables or the greater amount of stock. Somewhere within all of these you'll find the perfect Hot and Sour Soup for you. Steve and I make ours by tasting.*

**6-10 dried black Chinese or Japanese mushrooms**

**8-16 dried lily buds (also called golden needles)**

**1/8-1/4 cup dried cloud ears (also called tree ears or black fungus)**

**1-2 pieces whole canned bamboo shoots (the winter variety is best, as they are firmer and more flavorful)**

**2-3 squares dofu (the Chinese name for tofu or bean curd)**

**1/2 pound lean pork tenderloin**

**2-3 quarts rich chicken stock**

**1 1/2 teaspoons salt**

**2 or more tablespoons soy sauce**

**5 or more tablespoons white vinegar**

**1 teaspoon-1 tablespoon ground white pepper**

**1 tablespoon sesame oil, or to taste**

**3 tablespoons cornstarch, dissolved in 4 1/2 tablespoons cold water**

**2 lightly beaten eggs**

**3 scallions, chopped**

Soak the mushrooms, lily buds and cloud ears *separately* in about 1 cup of hot water for each dried ingredient. Leave about 30 minutes until soft. Drain the bamboo shoots and rinse them in cold water. Cut across the wedge into thin triangles, then shred into 1/4-inch strips. Drain the bean curd, rinse gently and cut into julienne strips about 1/3 inch by 1/3 inch by 3 inches. Set them aside carefully; they break easily. Cut the pork into strips the same size as the bean curd.

Drain the soaked dry ingredients when they are tender. Reserve the liquid from the mushrooms and the lily buds for the soup. (Discard the cloud ear water; it's too dirty to use in the soup.) Remove any hard stems or ends and gently squeeze out any remaining water. Shred the soaked vegetables. Shred the lily buds by tearing them apart lengthwise.

Pour the stock and the reserved soaking liquids into a large soup pot. Add the salt, soy sauce, vegetables and pork. Bring to a boil over high heat. Reduce to low heat, cover and simmer for 5 to 10 minutes. Add the vinegar, pepper and sesame oil to taste, and then bring to a boil again over high heat. (The soup can be prepared in advance to this point and refrigerated. When you are ready, reheat it and proceed.)

Add the bean curd to the soup. Combine the cornstarch with the water and slowly stir the mixture into the soup (be careful not to break up the bean curd). Stir until the soup thickens.

Pour the beaten eggs into the soup in a slow, steady stream, stirring as you pour. Adjust the seasonings (thin beads of perspiration should appear on your upper lip, even if you have a moustache, when this is just right!). Pour into a warm soup tureen and sprinkle with chopped scallions before serving.

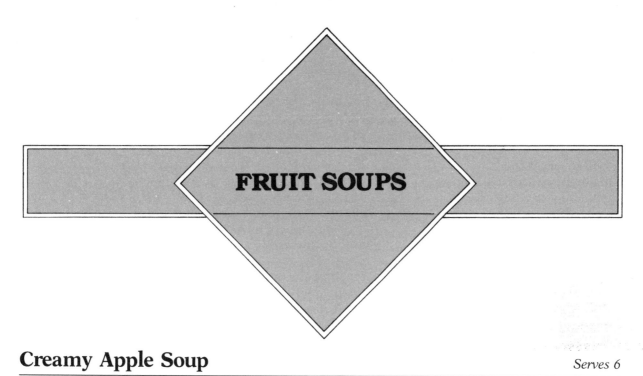

# FRUIT SOUPS

## Creamy Apple Soup

*Serves 6*

*When Autumn turns New England hills aflame with color, the smell of apples fills the air. I created this soup in memory of a log fire in a New Hampshire house set on a windswept hill.*

**2 pounds tart apples**
**Juice of half a lemon**
**4 tablespoons unsalted butter**
**4 cups finely chopped onions**
**4 cups rich chicken stock**
**¼ teaspoon powdered ginger**
**⅛ teaspoon freshly grated nutmeg**
**Salt and freshly ground pepper**
   **to taste**
**1 pint heavy cream**
**Pinch of salt**
**4 tablespoons Calvados, apple**
   **brandy or bourbon**
**2 tablespoons chopped crystallized**
   **ginger (optional)**

Cut the apples in half and remove the seeds with a melon ball scoop. Cut the apples into moderately thin slices, leaving the skins on. Squeeze the lemon juice over the apple slices to keep them from turning brown.

Sauté the onions quickly in the butter over high heat. When they begin to get limp, add the apples to the pan, and cover with buttered parchment paper. This will act as a blanket over the apples, catching the condensation and basting them. Cover with a lid and cook over gentle heat until the apples have become soft; this will take 10 to 15 minutes. Stir in the chicken stock, add the spices, and taste for salt and pepper. Simmer for 15 to 20 minutes, uncovered, stirring occasionally. Put the soup through a food mill to remove the apple skins. Return to the pan and heat.

While it is heating, whip the cream until it has thickened and stir in the Calvados. Add a pinch of salt. Serve the soup in hot deep bowls or mugs and float the cream on top.

To gild the lily, scatter crystallized ginger over the cream.

# Cream of Chestnut Soup

*September in France and October in Italy are the times when chestnuts are found lying everywhere from forest roads to sunny parks. In Europe, chestnuts are not the elegant and scarce treats they are in this country, but are used for flour and soup, not reserved for dessert. This soup is very rich and should be served in small portions.*

**4 tablespoons butter**
**2 medium-size carrots, chopped**
**1 medium-size onion, chopped**
**1 leek, white part only, cleaned**
   **and chopped**
**¼ teaspoon dry thyme, crumbled**
**1 pound canned unsweetened**
   **chestnuts, no liquid**
**4 cups chicken stock**
**½ cup heavy cream**
**1½ cups milk**
**½ cup pale dry sherry or**
   **dry Madeira**
**Salt and pepper to taste**
**Small croutons (see page 68)**
**Fresh chives, chopped**

Heat the butter in a skillet. Add the carrots, onion, leek and thyme. Cook until limp. Add the chestnuts, and sauté for 5 minutes. Add the stock, cover, and simmer for another 10 minutes or until the chestnuts are soft. Puree the soup in a food processor or blender and then return it to the pan. Add the cream, milk and sherry and heat through. Add salt and pepper to taste.

Float the croutons in each individual soup bowl and sprinkle lightly with fresh chives.

NOTE: Horse chestnuts *cannot* be substituted. They are poisonous!

# Cold Strawberry Soup

*My husband loves the strawberry jam from Alois Dallmayr in Munich. It has inspired this cold strawberry soup. Perfect on a hot June day, as refreshing as kir, this soup can also be served over ice.*

**Sugar syrup made from ½ cup**
   **water and ½ cup sugar, heated**
   **until the sugar has completely**
   **dissolved**
**4 cups fresh, ripe, cold strawberries**
**2 cups Rhine wine, chilled**
**4 tablespoons fresh lemon juice**
**Grated zest of 2 lemons**
**2 teaspoons Angostura bitters**
**Decoration: 1 cup plain yogurt;**
   **8 tiny rose-geranium leaves or**
   **8 fresh mint leaves**

Prepare the sugar syrup and allow it to cool. Refrigerate. Puree the cold strawberries in a food processor or blender. Add all the remaining ingredients to the processor and blend. Add the cold sugar syrup and blend again.

Serve this soup in an iced champagne "flute" with a tiny fillip (½ tablespoon) of yogurt floating on top. Decorate the yogurt with the fresh leaves.

# Danish Bridal Soup

*Serves 6*

*Some years ago I came across a recipe for "Bridal Pudding," a pure white confection topped with a bright yellow rum sauce and strawberries. I was living in the Danish countryside at the time and having survived the long, dark winter, marveled at the gorgeous and intoxicatingly fragrant freesias blooming outside my kitchen window. That dessert reminded me of those flowers and so I created this buttermilk-based soup. I serve it at showers and weddings and the guests seem to love it as much as I loved the freesias.*

**6 tablespoons sugar**
**2 egg yolks**
**1 tablespoon lemon juice**
**1 quart buttermilk**
**1 cup heavy cream, whipped, or**
  **1 cup crème fraîche (see page 15)**
**1 tablespoon almond slivers, toasted**
**6 strawberries cut into fans and**
  **spread slightly**

Whisk together the sugar and yolks until very thick and mousse-like. Stir in the lemon juice and then slowly add the buttermilk, whisking all the while.

Serve in cold bowls with a generous topping of whipped cream, and decorate each bowl with almonds and a strawberry fan.

# Brandied Peach Soup

*When I moved to Michigan I discovered, to my surprise and delight, that it was a leading peach-producing state. Peaches and nectarines were so abundant that I found myself continually cooking and developing recipes for them. This recipe was one of the most delightful to arise.*

**6 cups peaches, blanched and peeled**
   **(see page 14)**
**⅓ cup lemon juice**
**Pinch of salt**
**Pinch of mace**
**⅓ cup Cognac or brandy**
**Pinch of sugar (optional)**
**Decoration: Slices of peach, cut**
   **paper-thin; fresh mint sprigs**

Cut the peaches into quarters and puree them in a food processor or with a food mill. Add the lemon juice, salt, mace and brandy. Stir to combine. Drain through a fine sieve for a velvety texture or, if you prefer, allow the puree to stay slightly coarse.

This soup should be served immediately, as it separates when standing. Decorate each serving with paper-thin peach slices arranged in a flower pattern with a sprig of mint alongside.

---

## COLD FRUIT SOUP VARIATIONS

There are many fruits that can be treated like the peaches in Brandied Peach Soup to produce divine cold soups. For example, try:

• Canteloupe pureed with lemon juice, port and ½ teaspoon freshly grated ginger

• Honeydew melon with lime juice, vodka and 2 teaspoons orange-flower water

• Watermelon with lemon juice, gin and 2 teaspoons rose water

• Nectarines, lemon juice, white wine and a drop or two of Amaretto to taste

# Salads

# Preparing Salads

A basic and superb salad is dependent on a few things: perfectly fresh ingredients, good oil, good vinegar and a light touch. Fresh ingredients are available all year long. In summer the Farmers' Markets here in Michigan (and I hope everywhere else, too) overflow with a multitude of lettuces, a voluptuous variety of tomatoes and bushels of different types of cucumbers. Home gardens brim with zucchinis, nasturtium leaves ripen for picking, and sugar snap peas and long green beans can be plucked at their tender, crunchy best. We have fresh mushrooms year round and sweet carrots, oranges and apples, and our enlightened supermarkets now feature kale, celery root and three colors of grapes even through our fiercest blizzards. So whether you dress your salad the magnificently simple Italian way with a drizzle of olive oil to protect the texture of the greens, a pinch of salt to heighten their flavor, and a sprinkle of red wine vinegar to waken the taste buds or in a more complex manner, here are some ideas for splendid salads and delightful salad dressings.

## Leafy Greens to Use in Salads

Lettuce has been eaten by civilized people since at least 300 B.C., but for some reason belonged only to the home gardener until as late as the 20th century, when it became commercially important. Now, many different salad greens are available in addition to lettuce, and new varieties are being developed each year.

BOSTON lettuces are soft, small round heads of leaves that do not form a very tight head. The pale green leaves are sweet and have a rather buttery texture. While this is one of the most exquisitely delicate lettuces to choose from, it wilts quickly and has no longevity in the salad bowl. A salad containing this sort of lettuce should be served seconds after being dressed.

BIBB heads are similar to Boston heads, though smaller and even more delicate, and can vary from pale green to dark green. These leaves, too, are very fragile.

BELGIAN ENDIVE, small white spears of crisp, waxen beauty, lends elegance to salad. There is always a place for endives at a formal dinner.

CHICORY is also known as curly endive and can be identified by its feathery, curly bright green leaves that hold dressing well. This sharp tasting green mixes well with more delicate leaves.

ESCAROLE, second cousin to chicory, has broad

crinkle-edged leaves which are white at the bottom and darker green at the top. The stems of escarole are slightly bitter and they should be used judiciously mixed with more subtle lettuces.

LAMBS QUARTERS, ROCKET, and PURSLANE grow wild in fields and on lawns. They are piquant and delicious with a radishlike bite, and make a delightful addition to a green salad, but beware of overusing them.

LEAF LETTUCE may be light green, green tinged with red, or dark ruby red. Buy these lettuces whenever they are available. Crisp, yet tender, flavorful and without bitterness, they are welcome at any meal. Here in Michigan we are blessed with a wide variety of leaf lettuce that is available through most of the year.

ROMAINE, known in some parts of the country as "cos," is an ancient lettuce of the Aegean. It is a long, slightly cylindrical head of crunchy dark green leaves with white ribs. Add Romaine for a nice tangy flavor and its ability to stand up well as a garnish under more substantial salads or when salad needs to be made ahead.

SPINACH has a thick, firm, fresh leaf, which, when washed and dried well, adds a refreshing taste to a salad. Visually, it may add just the required finishing touch to your dish. Whenever possible, buy spinach loose and out of the bag.

WATERCRESS has deep green leaves with a peppery quality that add a nice piquant touch. Keep watercress stored head side down in a bowl of water in your refrigerator and enjoy the leaves and crisp stems for days and days.

NASTURTIUM leaves and blossoms, which also have a slightly peppery flavor, should not be overlooked. They add a delightful edible surprise to salads, as do other herbs and their blossoms.

## Assembling Salads

When preparing a salad, choose a variety of leafy greens to form its backbone. High in vitamins C and A, greens of all sorts offer crunchiness, tang, color and sweetness. Select crisp, lively-looking greens with a minimum of wilted outside leaves. Keep in mind, also, that the flavors, variety of texture and color should be compatible.

Wash the greens carefully in cold water, dunking the head or leaves several times, and change the water as often as necessary to remove all the dirt. Dry thoroughly with paper towels or in a salad spinner and place the leaves in the refrigerator between layers of paper towel until you are ready to use them.

When you are ready to assemble the salad, tear the fresh, dry greens into manageable-sized pieces. You may want to add some other ingredients to your salad now, which, when you're selecting them, will need an equal amount of forethought for compatibility and freshness. These days, rubbery cucumbers, curling carrot slices, quarters of wet tomato and the inevitable sad sliver of radish have been replaced by fresher equivalents and such innovative additions as thinly sliced raw cauliflower, raw mushrooms or zucchini. People have also found that a couple of spoonfuls of chopped cooked beets, added at the last minute, can create a sparkle. Indeed, each of these alone, dressed with a Vinaigrette, makes a fine salad, free from the strictures of routine.

But why stop there when orange sections, roasted red peppers, sliced artichoke bottoms and toasted pine nuts can be added, too? And with all caution now tossed to the wind, try toasting walnuts or sesame seeds for your salad, or adding squash blossoms or violets. Add cheeses and bacon crumbs, add marigolds, add croutons rubbed with garlic or lemon rind, and behold—Heaven fills the salad bowl.

# SALAD DRESSINGS

Sometimes the seemingly simplest things are really the trickiest to prepare. Salad dressings have few ingredients compared with tortes or casseroles, yet sheer terror can strike the cook who does not know the rules. There is certainly no lack of recipes, for directions for making salads and salad dressings have existed for centuries, and basically they have changed little. Also, though it appears that there are hundreds of recipes, all are variations of either Vinaigrette or Mayonnaise.

An early Vinaigrette recipe from 14th-century England reads:

> *SALAT: take parsel, sawge, garlec, chibollas, leeks, myntes, fenel, ton tressis [watercress] . . . waishe hem clene . . . myng hem wel with rawe oil. lay one vinegar and salt and serve it forth.*

When it is made just right, French Vinaigrette will always be a hit. When made without care, the result will be an oily, sodden mass of lettuce and platefuls of leftovers. The line is thin, but the lesson is simple. I have heard it takes four people to make a Vinaigrette: You need a spendthrift for the oil, a miser for the vinegar, a counselor for the salt, and a madman to stir it all about. All that is really required is a bowl, a whisk and some readily available ingredients: garlic, salt, mustard, oil, vinegar, pepper and herbs.

Ten years ago, the choices were simple. We chose a white or red wine vinegar, Dijon mustard and a salad oil or olive oil. Today, we can choose between white wine, red wine, champagne, sherry, blueberry, marigold, banana or nutmeg vinegars and between hazelnut, walnut, peanut, grapeseed, almond, corn and a huge variety of olive oils. We have a choice of mustards: green peppercorn, pink peppercorn, orange, lime and honey mustards as well as grainy mustards and a variety of Dijon mustards. Hundreds of vinaigrettes can be created to suit your salad with the following basic recipe.

# French Vinaigrette

*The measurements in this recipe are really not important. The secret of a beautiful salad dressing has to do with the delicate balance of flavors that taste good to you and the knowledge that the perfect proportions for a Vinaigrette are three parts oil to one part vinegar; the rest is imagination.*

**1 fat garlic clove, mashed to a paste
  with about ½ teaspoon salt
2 tablespoons Dijon mustard
1 cup virgin olive oil
⅓ cup white wine vinegar
1 teaspoon fresh thyme, or
  ½ teaspoon dried
Salt and pepper to taste**

Add the garlic paste to the mustard and stir. Pour in the oil and whisk until the dressing has become quite thick. The mustard acts as an emulsifier in this dressing and not only thickens it, but makes it fairly stable as well. Now whisk in your vinegar, herbs, salt and pepper. Taste the dressing. If it tastes a bit oily, *don't* add vinegar; if it tastes a bit vinegary, *don't* add oil. First add a bit more salt! Usually this brings everything together. Now taste for balance. You should not taste just garlic or just mustard. You should not really taste the oil or the vinegar, and the herbs should be just like perfume: heady and seductive, not overpowering and brazen. This is the essence of a perfect dressing to be used with lettuce, vegetables, fish, meat, pasta, rice or whatever the imagination devises.

To make the dressing thicker, add a beaten egg and whisk until thick. To make Roquefort Vinaigrette, add ½ cup crumbled Roquefort to 1 cup Vinaigrette, just before serving, and whisk gently. To make Avocado Vinaigrette, peel a ripe avocado, mash the flesh into a puree with a fork, add to 1 cup Vinaigrette, and whisk until smooth. Season with either ⅛ teaspoon Tabasco sauce or ¼ teaspoon nutmeg.

# Creamy Herb Vinaigrette

⅓ cup sour cream
1 cup Vinaigrette
3 tablespoons chopped fresh chives
2 tablespoons chopped fresh parsley
2 tablespoons chopped fresh basil
Salt and freshly ground pepper

Stir the sour cream into the vinaigrette and add the chopped herbs. Stir to combine. Add salt and pepper to taste.

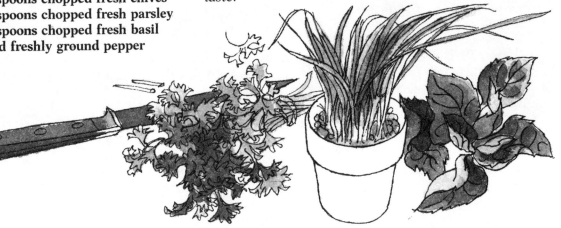

# El Prado

*Makes scant ½ cup*

*Try this Spanish twist on Vinaigrette on a chicory and honeydew melon or canteloupe salad.*

¼ cup walnut oil
3 tablespoons sherry vinegar
Salt and freshly ground pepper
    to taste
¼ cup toasted walnuts, coarsely
    chopped

Mix together all the ingredients except the walnuts. Dress the salad lightly and sprinkle with the nuts just before serving.

# Tangy Yogurt Dressing

*Makes 1¼ cups*

1 cup plain yogurt
2 cloves garlic, mashed
2 tablespoons fruity olive oil
Salt and pepper to taste

Mix all the ingredients together and allow to blend in the refrigerator for at least 1 hour. Remove the garlic cloves and serve the dressing on any tossed salad or precooked cold vegetables.

# CREAMY DRESSINGS

*Think of these as variations on a classic Vinaigrette, with the cream or yogurt taking the place of the oil.*

## Sour Cream Dressing

1 tablespoon sugar
2 tablespoons tarragon vinegar
½ teaspoon salt
1 cup sour cream

Mix the sugar, vinegar and salt together. Stir the mixture into the sour cream and allow to stand for at least 1 hour before using.

This dressing is excellent on sliced crisp cucumbers, fresh raw mushrooms, sliced—or, if luck has been on your side as a mushroom hunter, try stirring in ½ pound of fresh morels.

## Heavy Cream Dressing

*Makes 1½ cups*

3 tablespoons lemon juice
½ teaspoon grated lemon rind
½ teaspoon sugar
1 teaspoon salt
1 cup heavy cream, slightly
　thickened by whisking
1½ teaspoons dried herbs or
　1 tablespoon finely chopped
　fresh herbs

Mix the lemon juice, rind, sugar and salt together and stir into the slightly thickened cream. Add the herbs and allow to stand, refrigerated, for 1 hour before using. This is an excellent dressing for fish or vegetable salads.

VARIATION: Delete the herbs and add 2 tablespoons honey or pomegranate juice. Use on fruit salads.

## Spicy Yogurt Dressing

½ cup plain yogurt
1 hard-boiled egg yolk, mashed
2 tablespoons lemon juice
2 tablespoons chopped parsley
2 drops Tabasco sauce
Salt and pepper to taste

Mix all the ingredients together and serve on fruit or chicken salads, fish or turkey.

# SLIGHTLY SWEET DRESSINGS

## Pralines and Cream

*Makes 1½ cups*

½ cup sour cream or crème fraîche
½ cup heavy cream, lightly whipped
2 tablespoons lime juice
1½ tablespoons sugar
¼-½ cup pecans, lightly toasted and
　coarsely chopped
Pepper to taste

Place the sour cream in a medium-sized bowl and stir in the whipped cream, lime juice and sugar. Taste for tartness. Add the pecans and a small grinding of pepper. Taste again for balance and adjust the seasonings to please yourself.

For a superb blending of flavors, drizzle this over a summer salad of peaches and strawberries.

## Athena

*Makes ½ cup*

*Romaine, orange sections and thinly sliced purple onions combine intriguingly with this boiled, sweet dressing.*

3 tablespoons honey
¾ cup white wine tarragon vinegar
½ teaspoon orange-flower water
Salt and pepper to taste
Water to dilute the vinegar, if
　necessary

Bring the honey and the vinegar to a boil in a small saucepan. Boil for 1 minute, then allow to cool slightly. Add the orange-flower water, salt and pepper. If the vinegar has become too acidic in the course of cooking, dilute the dressing as necessary with water. Cool completely before using.

## Creamy Brandy Dressing

*Makes ½ cup*

½ cup heavy cream or yogurt
1 tablespoon Cognac or brandy
Pinch of sugar
Pinch of salt

Stir all the ingredients together and allow to stand in the refrigerator for 1 hour to mellow. This dressing should be served over fruit.

## Sweet Yogurt Dressing

*Makes ¾ cup*

1 tablespoon honey
1 teaspoon lime juice
2 teaspoons finely chopped fresh
　mint or 1 teaspoon rose water
½ cup plain yogurt

Mix the honey, lime juice and mint or rose water together until the honey has thinned. Stir the mixture into the yogurt and serve over fruit.

# Mayonnaise

*I have always been intrigued by how things were named, but the origin of Mayonnaise remains something of a mystery. Lyonnaise (as in potatoes) originated in Lyon, and Dijonnaise near Dijon, but it seems that Mayonnaise is an orphan. Although it is the most widely accepted French sauce or dressing, the base for countless other cold sauces, and the most popular of all additions to sandwiches and hors d'oeuvres, the place of its birth seems not to have been recorded. Perhaps its name is derived from* moyeu, *the old French word for egg yolk, or the French verb* manier—"to knead."

*Whatever its name may mean, Mayonnaise is well worth making by hand. For this recipe, make sure all the ingredients are at room temperature; it can easily be multiplied up to six egg yolks.*

**FOR EACH EGG YOLK, ADD:**
**2 teaspoons lemon juice or vinegar**
**Salt and pepper to taste**
**1 teaspoon Dijon mustard**
**Up to 1 cup oil (I use 3 parts corn oil and 1 part olive oil)**

Good mayonnaise may be made easily in the food processor, the mixer, or with a whisk or fork. If you choose to do this by hand, set your bowl on a wet dish towel so that the bowl will not move around. Mix the egg yolk with the lemon juice or vinegar and the salt and pepper. Beat in the Dijon mustard and, very slowly, start adding the oil, a drop at a time, with the measuring cup held in your left hand while whisking with your right (unless, of course, you're left-handed, in which case reverse the above).

Continue until the mayonnaise has become very thick. After the first ½ cup of oil has been absorbed you can start to add the oil a little faster in a thin stream. But that one little yolk will absorb all of the oil *only* if you "stretch" it very slowly. If the mayonnaise begins to thin, stop.

If your mayonnaise *does* break (curdle), don't despair—it can be fixed by either of these methods:

Put another room-temperature egg yolk in a clean bowl. Following the same procedure as before, drizzle in up to ½ cup of oil, a drop or two at a time. When it thickens, gradually stir in the curdled mayonnaise, tablespoon by tablespoon. Or, put a tablespoon of Dijon mustard into a bowl and keep dripping in half tablespoons of the curdled sauce until all the mayonnaise is returned to the new mixture and becomes smooth again.

Thin a mayonnaise that is too thick with a tablespoon or two of hot water, stock, tomato juice or fruit juice, as appropriate.

## Curried Mayonnaise

*Makes 2 cups*

1½ teaspoons curry powder
2 cups Mayonnaise

Blend the curry powder *thoroughly* into the mayonnaise—there must be no powdery bits left for a guest's tongue to find. Use as a binder for chicken salad.


## Pink Mayonnaise (Sauce Rosé)

*Makes 2½ cups*

⅓ cup tomato puree
Juice of 1 lemon or lime
1 teaspoon grated lemon or lime rind
2 cups Mayonnaise
Salt and pepper to taste

Add the tomato puree, citrus juice and rind to the mayonnaise. Stir to combine and then correct the seasonings. This is an excellent accompaniment for shrimp or crab.


## Green Mayonnaise (Sauce Verte)

*Makes 2 cups*

1½ cups Mayonnaise
1 tablespoon fresh chervil or
    tarragon or 1 teaspoon dried
2 teaspoons chopped fresh dill
    weed or ¾ teaspoon dried
2 tablespoons minced fresh chives
¼ cup fresh spinach, washed, dried
    and finely chopped in the food
    processor
¼ cup fresh watercress,
    washed, dried and finely
    chopped in the food processor
Salt and pepper to taste

Add the other ingredients to the mayonnaise in a large bowl. Stir until all the ingredients are well combined. Taste for salt and pepper. Serve on small pieces of freshly poached fish for an elegant, simple seafood salad.

# Horseradish Mayonnaise

*Makes 2½ cups*

1½ tablespoons grated horseradish
½ cup heavy cream, whipped
1 tablespoon lemon juice
2 teaspoons Worcestershire sauce
1 cup Mayonnaise

Fold all the ingredients together and serve on cold roast beef.

# Lemon or Orange Mayonnaise

*Makes 2 cups*

Juice of 2 lemons or 1 large orange
Grated rind of 1 lemon or 1 orange
2 tablespoons good port, if using
   orange juice
1½ cups thick Mayonnaise

Stir the citrus juice and rind into the mayonnaise. Add the port, if you have used orange juice. This dressing is particularly delicious on cold asparagus.

# Aioli (Garlic Mayonnaise)

*Makes 2½ cups*

3 large garlic cloves, mashed with
   ¼ teaspoon salt
2 cups Mayonnaise
1 tablespoon lemon juice
Freshly ground pepper
Hot water for thinning, if necessary

Add the well-mashed garlic to the mayonnaise and stir. Finish with the lemon juice and freshly ground pepper. If the aioli is too thick, thin it with a little hot water. Serve on cold vegetables or fish.

# VEGETABLE SALADS

## Asparagus Vinaigrette

*Serves 4-6 asparagus lovers or 8 normal humans*

*When the asparagus season comes to Michigan, we all stop what we're doing and eat asparagus. For years we've taught free half-hour classes on how to cook the elegant stalk. The restaurant heralds each returning season with an asparagus festival; a singular favorite is always this recipe.*

**2 pounds fresh asparagus**
**1 cup French Vinaigrette made with**
  **tarragon vinegar (see page 55)**
**Garnish: 2 hard-boiled egg yolks**
  **(save the whites and chop them**
  **for your next tossed salad)**

Snap off the tough ends of the asparagus stalks, just where they break easily. Wash in cold water and peel the stem only if the stalk is larger around than your pinkie, or if the spears are not at their peak. Steam the asparagus for 5 minutes, or blanch in plenty of boiling, lightly salted water. Cook for 5 minutes if you like your asparagus crunchy, for 8 minutes if you prefer a slightly more tender consistency. Cool the spears immediately in cold water, but do not allow them to become too cold; they absorb dressing better while still a little warm. Drain well.

Pour the vinaigrette over the asparagus and allow to marinate for at least 1 hour. This salad can be made a day ahead to this point, and refrigerated.

Lay all the spears in the same direction on an oval platter. Just before serving, crumble the hard-boiled egg yolks into a bowl and spoon out in 3 strips across the base of the asparagus.

# Asparagus-Mushroom Salad

*Serves 6-8*

*Chinese tastes that influence me also influenced this salad. It needs no garnish, but looks most attractive on an Oriental plate.*

1 pound fresh young asparagus
½ pound fresh mushrooms, sliced
  (edible wild mushrooms do well)
2 scallions, coarsely chopped

DRESSING:
½ cup light olive oil
1 tablespoon white rice vinegar
2 tablespoons lemon juice
1 teaspoon sesame oil
½ teaspoon soy sauce
Freshly ground black pepper

Steam the asparagus for 5 minutes or blanch in plenty of boiling, salted water for 5 minutes. Remove the spears while still crunchy and immerse in cold water to stop the cooking. When they have cooled, cut them into 1-inch lengths and toss with the mushrooms and scallions.

While the asparagus is cooking, whisk together the remaining ingredients. Pour the dressing over the asparagus and marinate for 2 hours.

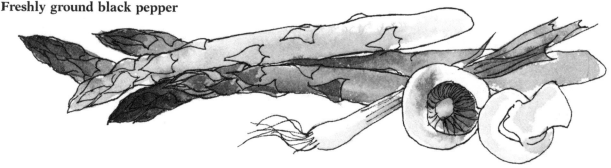

# Marinated Green Beans

*Serves 4-6*

1 pound fresh green beans
1 pimiento, oil packed
1 cup Vinaigrette (see page 55)
  made with cider vinegar, grainy
  mustard and a pinch of oregano
2 cloves garlic stuck on a toothpick

Blanch and cool the green beans. Trim to the same length and place in a narrow bowl. Slice the pimiento into thin strips and set aside on a paper towel to drain. Pour the dressing over the beans and toss well. Bury the skewered garlic amid the beans and set aside to marinate for 1 hour.

Remove the garlic by finding the toothpick and arrange little bundles of marinated beans on individual salad plates. Cross each bundle with 2 thin strips of pimiento and serve.

# Vegetables More Than à la Grecque

*Serves 8*

*Everywhere in the world people serve cold marinated vegetables. The technique usually demands little more than blanching the vegetables, cooling them in cold water and dressing them with a well-flavored Vinaigrette. Here is a variation on that theme. Try it with different flavors and different vegetables.*

½ cup olive oil
4 small onions, sliced in thin rounds
4 cups small carrots, cut in ½-inch
  thick rounds
3 cloves garlic, peeled
2 cups dry white wine
1 cup water
¼ cup lemon juice
6 tablespoons tomato paste
2 bay leaves broken in half
¼ cup whole coriander seeds
2 1-inch-by-2-inch strips lemon
  peel
2 1-inch-by-2-inch strips orange
  peel
1½ teaspoons salt
¼ teaspoon coarsely ground pepper
1 medium-size head snow white
  cauliflower, washed and separated
  into florets
½ cup chopped fresh parsley

Heat the oil in a large saucepan. Add the onions, carrots and garlic. Cover and cook gently for 5 minutes, making sure that the vegetables do not take on color. Add the wine, water, lemon juice and tomato paste. Stir to combine. Add the bay leaves, coriander seeds, citrus peels and salt and pepper. Cover and bring to a boil. Add the cauliflower, return the lid and simmer until the cauliflower is tender but still slightly crisp.

Remove the vegetables to a bowl, using a slotted spoon, and place in the refrigerator. Boil the liquid rapidly to reduce it to 2 cups. Remove the bay leaves. Pour this marinade over the cold vegetables. Chill for several hours. Toss with fresh parsley and serve.

# Cabbage Salad

*This is a good salad to munch as a snack instead of popcorn, and a lot better for you.*

1 medium-size head green cabbage,
  quartered and cored
1 small head red cabbage, quartered
  and cored
2 cucumbers, peeled
2 large carrots, peeled
½ large sweet purple onion
½ large sweet white onion

DRESSING:
8 tablespoons corn oil
¼ cup sugar
¾ cup white wine vinegar
4 tablespoons water
4 teaspoons salt

Cut both types of cabbage into ¼-inch shreds. Cut cucumbers in half lengthwise and then into ½-inch slices. Cut the carrots on the diagonal, into slices ¼ inch thick. Slice the onions thinly.

Whisk all the dressing ingredients together in a large bowl. Add the prepared vegetables and mix well. Refrigerate for a couple of hours before serving.


# Mushrooms and Cream

2 pounds fresh mushrooms, sliced

DRESSING:
2 tablespoons lemon juice
1 tablespoon dry white wine
½ teaspoon lemon rind
¼ teaspoon sugar
½ teaspoon salt
1 tablespoon Italian parsley
1 teaspoon dried dill weed, or
  1 tablespoon fresh
1 cup cream, thickened slightly by
  whisking

Mix all the ingredients for the dressing and pour over the sliced mushrooms. Stir gently. Marinate for at least 2 hours before serving.

# FOUR CHINESE SALADS

*During the summer that I studied in Taiwan with a group of cooking school teachers, food writers and other Chinese food enthusiasts, we were introduced to a vast number of entirely new dishes. We were surprised at the number of pickles or cold salads we were served. Here are four improvisations inspired by restaurants in Taipei.*

## Vegetable Salad (Hunan)

*Serves 8 with other first courses in a typical Chinese meal*

½ pound mixed vegetables
  (shredded bok choy, sliced white
  mushrooms, asparagus tips or
  other vegetables)
3 tablespoons medium-strength
  soy sauce
4 tablespoons rice wine vinegar
2 tablespoons sesame oil
1 tablespoon hot pepper oil
1 teaspoon brown sugar
2 tablespoons peanut oil
1 tablespoon finely minced ginger
1 tablespoon finely minced garlic
1 tablespoon minced scallion
1 tablespoon Chinese wine or
  dry sherry
1 tablespoon Chinese coriander
  (cilantro) leaves
1½ cups chicken stock

Toss all the ingredients together and serve well chilled.

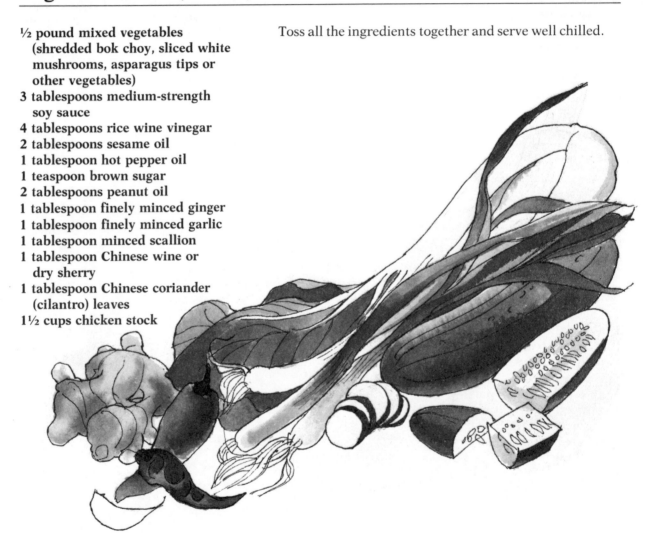

# Chinese Pickles (Ma La Hwong Gua—Szechuan) *Serves 8 as above*

1½ pounds long, thin, "burpless" cucumbers
1 tablespoon salt
10 slices ginger, shredded
1 fresh hot red pepper, shredded
¼ cup sesame oil
1 teaspoon Szechuan peppers
3 dried hot red peppers cut into 1-inch pieces
2½ tablespoons rice vinegar
2 tablespoons sugar

Remove the cucumber tips, leaving the cucumbers unpeeled. Cut each in half lengthwise and then horizontally into at least 8 sections. Mix with salt and allow to stand for 30 minutes. Rinse in cold water and drain. Place the cucumbers in a bowl and sprinkle with ginger and fresh red pepper.

Heat a wok, small skillet or small sauté pan; add the sesame oil. Stir-fry the Szechuan peppers over moderate heat until they are fragrant. Add the hot red peppers and stir-fry briefly. (Stand back—the fumes are potent!) Pour the oil and peppers over the cucumbers, add the vinegar and sugar. Refrigerate for at least 6 hours or overnight.

NOTE: This dish becomes hotter and hotter as it sits!

# Pickled Red Radishes (Yeh Sho Chong Lau Bo) *Serves 8 as above*

20 red radishes, cut into fans
1 teaspoon salt
2 tablespoons sugar
1 tablespoon rice wine vinegar
½ teaspoon salt, if necessary

Sprinkle the radishes with the salt. Allow to stand for 30 minutes. Wash the radishes well and press out the water. Add the sugar, vinegar, the remaining ½ teaspoon salt, if necessary, and toss well. Chill for at least 3 hours. Serve cold.

# Celery with Mustard (Dzia Moa Tsing-Tsai—Peking) *Serves 8*

1½ pounds very white celery (all hearts, if possible)
3 tablespoons Dijon mustard
2 tablespoons warm water
½ teaspoon salt
½ teaspoon sugar
1 cup chicken broth
1 teaspoon cornstarch
Soy sauce to taste

Cut the celery into thin fingers about 2 inches long. Blanch in boiling water for a minute, or just until tender. Drain and stop the cooking by rinsing the celery in cold water.

Mix the mustard with the water. Bring the salt, sugar, broth and cornstarch to a boil; add the mustard mixture, cool, and pour over the celery. Serve warm or cool, preceding a Chinese meal.

# Woodbine Dressing for Caesar Salad

*Serves 8*

*Outside the New Hampshire town where I grew up is a restaurant that attracts almost as many summer visitors as spring-fed Lake Sunapee, close by, with its mountain, pine woods and deep blue sky, given to multiple rainbows. The Woodbine Cottage, run by Eleanor and Robert Hill, is a gem of a place, surrounded by flower gardens and as fragrant with good smells within as without. The Hills' special salad dressing, a thick mayonnaisey version of the classic Caesar Salad dressing, is one of the best I know, and I thank them for sharing it. They use broken curly endive and leaf lettuce for their Caesar Salad, and you may like to, too.*

1 egg
¾ cup salad oil
¼ cup lemon juice
1 teaspoon salt
½ teaspoon black pepper
1 teaspoon Worcestershire sauce
¼ cup grated Parmesan cheese
Garnish: ¾ cup garlic croutons
  (see below)

Submerge the egg in boiling water for 1 minute, then break it into a bowl and whip until fluffy. Continue beating at high speed, slowly adding the oil. Reduce the speed and add the remaining dressing ingredients.

Dress the salad greens plentifully and serve in individual bowls, garnished with croutons.

## GARLIC CROUTONS

1 loaf good white bread (homemade,
  if possible), trimmed of crust
¼-½ pound unsalted butter
2 cloves garlic, finely chopped

Cut the bread in thick slices and allow them to dry slightly. Cut ½-inch fingers from each slice and then crosscut into ½-inch cubes. Heat part of the butter and a little chopped garlic in an omelette or frying pan and, using a handful at a time, fry the cubes slowly until they are crisp and golden. Add more butter and garlic as you need it.

NOTE: You can substitute herbs for the garlic, or serve the croutons plain, or cut in decorative shapes, if you like.

# Persian Cucumber and Yogurt Salad (Kasik)

*Serves 4-6*

*I have served this salad as a first course before a spicy meal, as a* raita *in an Indian meal, as a palate cleanser between courses, and have happily carried it to work as lunch. It is very simple to make, and by adding four cups of ice-cold buttermilk, you can also turn it into an unusual soup. Be sure the bowls are iced!*

2 cucumbers, peeled and finely
  chopped
4 scallions, chopped
2 sprigs fresh mint, chopped
2 sprigs fresh basil, chopped
3 cups plain yogurt
¼ cup walnuts
½ cup dry currants
½ teaspoon salt

Add all the vegetables and herbs to the yogurt. Stir. Add the walnuts, currants and salt. Stir again and taste for flavor. Serve very cold.


# Cucumber and Raspberry Salad

*Serves 8*

*Sometimes eating a dish that falls below expectations is a far better learning experience than enjoying one that meets them. I once ordered a salad in a restaurant that conjured up such an incredible image that I was already tasting it long before it arrived. When it was set before me, my hopes were dashed—and I hurried home to create the one I had been dreaming about.*

½ cup light, fruity olive oil
3 tablespoons raspberry vinegar
Salt and freshly ground black
  pepper
3 tablespoons crème fraîche
  (see page 15)
4 cucumbers, peeled and thinly
  sliced
3 tablespoons chopped fresh chives
½ pint fresh raspberries
8 sprigs mint

Whisk the oil into the vinegar. Add salt and pepper to taste. This will not be a stable emulsion until after the crème fraîche has been added, so don't worry if the mixture seems to want to separate. Whisk in the crème fraîche. Taste for balance of flavors.

Arrange the cucumber slices on individual salad plates in a slightly overlapping pattern. Dress lightly with the raspberry vinaigrette and sprinkle sparingly with the chives. Arrange 3 or 4 raspberries at the edge of each salad, and finish with a fresh mint sprig.

# Fine Upstanding Potato Salad

*Serves 6*

3 pounds potatoes, unpeeled
3 hard-cooked eggs, coarsely diced
1 cup diced celery
3 whole scallions, minced
½ cup frozen peas, defrosted but not
  cooked (of course, fresh are even
  better, provided they're small and
  sweet)
½ cup piccalilli or cabbage relish
1 large clove garlic, mashed
1 teaspoon celery seed
¾ cup Mayonnaise (see page 59)
¼ cup mustard
Salt and pepper to taste
Handful parsley, chopped

Boil the potatoes in salted water until just tender. Submerge in cold running water until they are cool enough to handle. Slip off the skins with a small paring knife. Return the potatoes to the cold water if the salad is to be made right away. If you have time, refrigerate them overnight.

When the potatoes are completely cold, dice them. Mix together all the other ingredients except the parsley and combine with the potatoes. Adjust the seasonings and toss with parsley just before serving.

# French Potato Salad

*Serves 6-8*

*The French have a charming and simple way of preparing potato salad. Once you've tasted it, you'll discover a new taste elevated far above the usual picnic food. This recipe typifies French everyday cooking; I once worked with a French chef who ate this salad every day for lunch!*

2 pounds small new potatoes
½ cup dry white wine
2 tablespoons chopped fresh parsley
2 tablespoons chopped fresh chives
1 tablespoon chopped fresh chervil
  or sweet woodruff
1 tablespoon minced shallots
½ cup olive oil
2½ tablespoons white wine vinegar
1 teaspoon Dijon mustard
Salt and plenty of fresh pepper

Scrub the potatoes, but do not peel them. Put them in a saucepan with sufficient cold water to cover; add 1 teaspoon of salt for each quart of water. Bring to a boil, cover and simmer for 10 to 15 minutes. When the potatoes are just tender, drain off the water and toss gently, over low heat, to remove the remaining moisture.

Pour the wine into a bowl and add the herbs. Cut the potatoes in half and add them to the wine. The warm potatoes will absorb the flavor of the wine as they cool. When the potatoes are cool, drain off any wine that may not have been absorbed.

Mix together the olive oil, vinegar, mustard and salt and pepper. Pour the dressing over the potatoes and toss gently, taking care not to break them. Serve warm or at room temperature.

NOTE: Large potatoes could be used in this recipe as well, though the flavor is not quite as exquisite. Put 2 pounds of unpeeled potatoes in cold salted water. Cover and simmer for 15 to 20 minutes after the water comes to a boil. Peel the potatoes, slice them into the white wine and proceed with the recipe.

# Tomato Salad with Cheese (Insalata Lipari) *Serves 4*

*I first encountered this salad on the Aeolian island of Lipari. It was served with a local fresh sheep's-milk cheese called Pecorino. The experience of that warm day on a volcanic island compelled me to re-create the recipe. You can vary this by using a French Vinaigrette dressing (see page 55) and calling it Salade Provençal.*

**2 large summer-ripe juicy tomatoes**
**1 Liparian Pecorino, or 1 log**
**of Montrachet goat cheese or**
**1 Buffula (fresh mozzarella with**
**part water buffalo milk)**
**Plenty (about ½ cup) of virgin**
**Italian olive oil**
**Freshly ground pepper, Tellicherry**
**peppercorns, if possible**

Slice the tomatoes about ⅓ inch thick. Slice the cheese slightly thinner than the tomatoes. Choose an attractive shallow dish and arrange the tomatoes alternately in overlapping slices with the cheese. Drizzle on the olive oil; don't be afraid to be a little heavy-handed here. Serve with freshly ground pepper—lots of it.

# MAIN-DISH SALADS

## Summer Salad in a "Bread Bowl"—For Michael
*Serves 4*

*Wine seems cheaper than water in France and I marvel at how freely the French make use of it. I have learned to wash strawberries in white wine, to serve peaches in a glass of cold red, and to enjoy tomatoes with the aromatic brandy known as Armagnac. Take this loaf off to the beach or on a picnic.*

1 round peasant loaf of French or
  Italian bread
¼ cup virgin olive oil
4 perfectly ripe tomatoes
1 pound medium-size to large
  shrimp, cooked and peeled (see
  page 15), (lump crabmeat or
  lobster, crayfish or even chicken
  could be substituted)
2 scallions, whites and greens,
  chopped
Salt and pepper to taste
2 teaspoons orange zest
2 teaspoons finely chopped fresh
  basil or fresh dill
2 tablespoons Armagnac

Cut off a lid from the loaf of bread and scoop out the soft interior, leaving a bowl-like shell. Sprinkle the inside lightly with some of the oil. Set aside. Cut the tomatoes into wedges and toss them with the shrimp, scallions, salt and pepper, orange zest and basil or dill. Sprinkle with the remaining olive oil and finally flavor the ingredients with Armagnac.

Pile the ingredients into the bread bowl and cover with the lid. Wrap in foil and refrigerate for 15 minutes before serving.

NOTE: Small individual salad/sandwiches are a novel idea. Use crisp French bread rolls and serve one to everyone. If you're not traveling far for your picnic, fill the rolls before you leave. If the salad will have to wait for more than 30 minutes, it is better to fill it just before serving.

# Cold Lobster and Pesto Salad

*Serves 4*

*Pure white lobster ringed with red, bright green pesto, and celadon-green cucumbers lend this handsome dish an Oriental air, though it is Tuscan in its inspiration. San Franciscan and fellow cooking school teacher Jack Lirio taught me how to make "noodles" by shaving long peeled cucumbers evenly from top to bottom with a cheese plane, then dropping the shavings into boiling salted water for a second or two to soften. You can also use a swivel peeler and just keep peeling, pressing down so that the noodles aren't too thin.*

**Cold cooked meat from 2 1½-pound lobsters, claws and tails**
**2 tablespoons olive oil**

**PESTO:**
**1½ cups fresh basil leaves, tightly packed**
**1 clove garlic**
**¼ cup pine nuts**
**¼ cup grated Parmesan**
**¼ cup olive oil**
**2-4 tablespoons white wine or chicken stock, for thinning**
**Salt, if necessary**

**Garnish: Cucumber noodles, cooked lobster coral or a tomato rose (see page 16)**

Prepare the pesto by placing the basil, garlic and pine nuts in a food processor or blender. Process for several seconds, add the cheese and process till blended. With the motor running, pour in the oil very slowly; by drops at the outset and then in a thin stream. The pesto will be very thick; thin with wine or broth to the desired consistency. Taste and add salt if necessary.

Slice the lobster meat into *very* thin oval slices and arrange them, overlapping, in concentric circles on a large round platter. Brush the olive oil over the top so that the slices glisten attractively. Spread a very thin stripe of pesto over each circle of lobster. Mound the cucumber noodles in the center, cover with the remaining pesto and garnish with coral or a tomato rose.

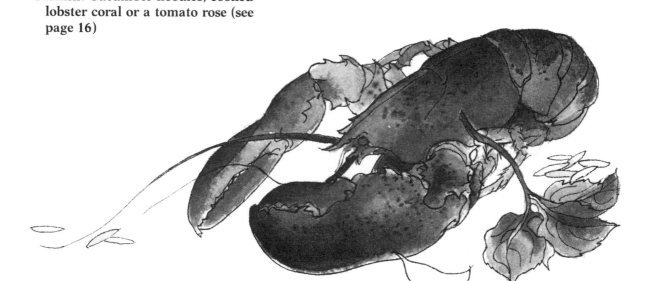

# EASY VARIATIONS ON SEAFOOD SALADS

## SHRIMP

Bind cooked cold shrimp and asparagus tips with just enough Green Mayonnaise (see page 60) to hold it all together.

## FISH

Poach 1-1½-inch pieces of firm-fleshed fish such as salmon, halibut or swordfish for 3 minutes in Court Bouillon (see page 23). Remove, drain and cool. Combine lightly with Curried Mayonnaise (see page 60) and serve on a bed of crisp cucumbers.

## SCALLOPS

Dress cold scallops with a French Vinaigrette (see page 55) made with lime juice. Add diced pimiento and a small amount of hot green chili, diced, for color and zip.

## MUSSELS

Toss cold leftover mussels with Mayonnaise (see page 59) and minced celery. Sprinkle lightly with finely chopped parsley before serving.

# Duck Salad with Oranges (Duckling à l'Orange)

*I try to teach my students that the inspiration for a recipe can come from almost anywhere. When you have mastered the basic techniques, it is safe to experiment with other combinations of ingredients. This salad is really a distant cousin to the classic Duckling à l'Orange, embroidered and enhanced by my enjoyment of casseroles made with duck and olives. I usually serve it with crisp deep-fried shoestring potatoes, called "Pommes Paille" in French. They make a good texture contrast.*

5-pound duck
2 medium-size carrots, halved
2 medium-size onions, quartered
4 bouquets garni (see page 15)
6 medium-size oranges, peeled and
    sectioned (see page 16)
1 cup sliced pitted black olives
2 small purple onions, thinly sliced
Salt
4 bunches watercress
Dark green lettuce leaves
Lemon Vinaigrette (recipe follows)
Garnish: ¼ cup sliced toasted
    almonds (toast for 10 minutes in a
    350-degree oven until lightly
    browned)

Put the duck into a deep pot, cover it with cold water and bring to a boil. Boil 4 to 5 minutes; remove the duck, pour off the water and wash the pot. This will remove as much fat as possible. Return the duck to the pot, cover it with fresh cold water and bring to a boil again. Skim it well. Add the carrots, onions and the bouquets garni. Reduce the heat, cover the pot and simmer slowly for 1 to 1½ hours, until the duck is tender. Drain.

Skin the duck and cut the meat into large pieces; combine with the orange sections, olives and onions. Sprinkle lightly with salt. Chill for 1 hour. Wash and dry the watercress; trim off the tough parts of the stems, leaving just about an inch. Just before serving, fold in the watercress.

Line a large salad bowl with lettuce leaves and pile the duck, watercress, oranges, olives and onions on top. Toss the salad lightly with dressing and garnish with toasted almonds. Serve at once.

## LEMON VINAIGRETTE

1 clove garlic
½ teaspoon salt
½ cup olive oil
4-6 tablespoons lemon juice, to taste
Large pinch rosemary, crushed with
    a mortar and pestle

Mash the garlic in the salt (see page 14). Blend with 2 tablespoons of the oil in a food processor or with a whisk. Add the remaining ingredients and the remaining oil and blend.

# Salat Oliviet (Chicken and Ham Salad)

*Serves 6-8*

*This famous salad was named after the French chef of Czar Nicholas II in an era when everything French— and especially food—was very much in vogue in Russia.*

**4 large whole chicken breasts, poached, skinned, cubed (see page 14)**
**8 medium-size carrots, peeled, parboiled till tender and diced**
**2 pounds potatoes, cooked, peeled and cubed**
**¼ pound cooked ham, cubed**
**1 cup dill pickles without garlic, diced**
**½ cup pimientos, diced**
**10 ounces fresh shelled peas or substitute frozen peas**
**1½ teaspoons salt**
**Freshly ground pepper**
**¼ cup lemon juice**
**2 tablespoons Dijon mustard**
**1 cup Mayonnaise (see page 59)**
**½ cup each pitted green and black olives, chopped**
**4 hard-cooked eggs (see page 13), quartered**

Prepare all the ingredients and set them aside. Do not cook the peas; if you are using frozen ones, just defrost them. Add the lemon juice and mustard to the mayonnaise and toss with all the other ingredients, adding the olives last. Season with salt and pepper and chill for 2 hours if possible. Serve surrounded with quarters of perfect hard-cooked eggs.

# Bon Bon Chicken (Banbanji)

*This is a most unusual salad—spectacular to present on an enormous platter at a Chinese banquet and perfect when you crave something cold and spicy. It offers a tantalizing combination of flavors and textures.*

2 whole chicken breasts (about
   1½-2 pounds)
6 scallions, 3 of them cut into 2-inch
   lengths
1-inch piece of fresh ginger, slivered
1½ teaspoons salt
1 tablespoon dry sherry or Chinese
   wine
1 tablespoon whole Szechuan
   peppercorns
2 cucumbers
2-ounce package cellophane noodles
Boiling water

DRESSING:
8 large cloves garlic
½ tablespoon hot pepper oil
1-inch piece ginger, finely chopped
2 teaspoons ground roasted
   Szechuan peppercorns
2 teaspoons sugar
1½ tablespoons sesame paste
4 teaspoons Chinese red vinegar (or
   substitute regular white vinegar)
2 tablespoons sesame oil
5 tablespoons soy sauce
2 tablespoons water

Garnish: Greens of 4 scallions, sliced
   so the "rings" are intact

Split the chicken breasts in half and place in a shallow bowl (a glass pie plate is ideal). Smash the 3 cut scallions with the broad side of a cleaver or a chef's knife. Slice the remaining 3 scallions into very thin slices and set aside. Combine the smashed scallions, ginger slivers, 1 teaspoon salt, sherry and peppercorns. Rub the mixture all over the chicken breasts. Marinate at room temperature for 1 hour, turning the chicken several times.

Peel the cucumbers and cut in half lengthwise. Scoop out the seeds and cut in thirds crosswise. Place the slices in a bowl and sprinkle with ½ teaspoon salt. Mix well and allow to "sweat" for about 30 minutes. Pour boiling water over the cellophane noodles and allow to soak for 20 minutes.

Steam the chicken in the plate for 30 minutes over boiling water. Remove and allow to cool in the refrigerator.

Bring several cups of water to a boil in a medium-sized saucepan. Drain the softened noodles and add them to the boiling water. Cook 2 to 3 minutes after the water returns to the boil. Drain the noodles, rinse in cold water and set aside.

Smash the garlic to remove the peel and place in a mortar. Add the pepper oil. Combine the finely chopped ginger with the garlic, oil and ½ teaspoon salt in the mortar and grind to a paste with the pestle. Remove to a larger bowl.

Dry roast the Szechuan peppercorns by heating and shaking them in a small dry pan until little wisps of smoke appear. Grind, using a mortar and pestle. Add the ground peppers, sugar, sesame paste, vinegar, sesame oil, soy sauce and water to the garlic mixture in the large bowl. Stir in the remaining chopped scallions, and continue to stir until the sauce is well blended.

Drain the cucumbers and arrange decoratively on a platter. Cut the cellophane noodles into smaller pieces to facilitate serving, and arrange atop the cucumbers. Skin the chicken and remove the meat from the bone. Chop into long strips, pick off any brown peppercorns adhering, and arrange on top of the noodles. Spoon the dressing over the dish just before serving and garnish with the scallion rings.

# Chicken Ravigote

RAVIGOTE DRESSING:
1 tablespoon each finely chopped
    chervil, chives, parsley, shallots
    and tarragon
1 tablespoon capers
¼ cup dry white wine
1 tablespoon lemon or lime juice
1 cup Mayonnaise (see page 59)

3 cups diced cooked chicken
4 hollowed-out tomatoes
1 hard-cooked egg white, chopped
2 tablespoons finely chopped fresh
    parsley

Combine all the dressing ingredients except the mayonnaise in a small pan and cook over low heat for 10 minutes. Cool, and then stir into the mayonnaise. Fold in the chicken. Pile into the tomato shells and serve, sprinkled with chopped egg white and parsley.

BEEF RAVIGOTE VARIATION: Toss 4 cups of thinly sliced cold, rare roast beef or steak with 1 cup of dressing and allow to mellow, refrigerated, for at least 3 hours before serving. Spread the beef in overlapping slices on a well-garnished plate of lettuce and serve with lots of crusty French bread.

# Cold Sliced Pork Salad

4 cups thinly sliced cold roast pork
¾ cup fruity olive oil, mixed with
    ¼ cup Balsamic vinegar
¾ cup chopped tart apples (Granny
    Smiths are excellent)
2 bunches watercress
Salt and pepper to taste

Marinate the pork in the oil and vinegar for 2 hours. Adjust the salt and pepper. Toss with the watercress and apples and serve with warm whole wheat bread and butter.

---

## POULTRY SALADS MADE FROM LEFTOVERS

• Toss pieces of cooked cold chicken cut in 1-inch pieces with walnuts, diced pears, chopped chives and enough mayonnaise to hold together. If this seems a bit heavy when tossed, lighten it with a couple of tablespoons of French Vinaigrette (page 55).

• Mix cubes of turkey meat with green seedless grapes and dress with Horseradish Mayonnaise (see page 61) for a zesty change of pace. Sprinkle with chopped chives before serving.

• Lightly dress pieces of leftover cold duck with equal parts of Mayonnaise (see page 59) and yogurt and a grating of fresh nutmeg. At the last minute, toss with a chiffonade of fresh spinach.

---

# Baked Chèvre (Goat Cheese) Salad *Serves 4*

*Here is a hot salad that is simple to prepare and delicious to eat. It is a favorite in our cooking classes that deal with Dinner in a Hurry. Experiment with different types of goat cheese. Try Montrachet, Bucheron or Lingot; Dolmen, Pyramide or Pave Jacquin are just as good!*

**½ pound chèvre or other goat
  cheese cut into ¾-inch slices**
**¾ cup walnut oil**
**1 cup lightly toasted very fine
  breadcrumbs**
**Assorted red-leaf lettuce leaves, as
  varied in color as possible**

Preheat the oven to 425 degrees.

Arrange the slices of cheese on a cookie sheet with sides, leaving an inch of space between each slice. Brush each slice lightly with the oil and dust liberally with breadcrumbs. Bake in the hot oven for about 3 minutes. Try not to let the cheese melt except around the edges.

Remove to lettuce-lined plates and serve at once with crispy French bread.

NOTE: You can vary this by using herb-flavored breadcrumbs, or mixing some finely grated lemon or orange peel with the crumbs; by substituting crushed black peppercorns, or finely chopped almonds or pistachios for the breadcrumbs; or by substituting for the walnut oil, olive oil flavored with ½ teaspoon crumbled herbs or your favorite Vinaigrette.

# SALADS MADE WITH GRAINS

Any starchy grain or vegetable (especially cold leftovers) can benefit from being drizzled with well-flavored Vinaigrette highlighted with assorted vegetables, mounded into a lettuce-lined bowl or a hollowed-out tomato, green pepper or artichoke, and topped off with appropriate garnishes.

The basic recipe for any cold grain salad is very simple: for every three cups of cold, cooked starchy grains add quarter to half a cup Vinaigrette (depending on how much the grain will absorb without becoming oily) and half a cup of "frills."

The grains and starchy vegetables can be cold rice, kasha or pasta; cooked flageolet, lentils or lima beans; kidney beans, Great Northern beans or any cold, cooked dried beans.

The Vinaigrette can be any of those on pages 55-56, as appropriate to the basic grain you are using.

The frills can be leftover peas, chopped fresh tomatoes, cucumbers, slant-sliced raw green beans . . . let your fancy roam, knowing that if you follow the formula, mix everything lightly with your hands and present your salad with a smile, it is bound to be a success.

# Cracked Wheat Salad (Tabbouleh)

*Serves 6-8*

*This cracked wheat or bulgur salad is a favorite with my vegetarian friends, and no wonder. Aromatic with Middle Eastern spices and glistening lightly with olive oil, it is fresh, chewy and filling without being heavy—perfect for a summer's evening.*

**1 cup bulgur (sometimes called burgul)**
**3 medium-size absolutely ripe tomatoes, blanched, peeled, seeded and chopped (see page 00)**
**1 cup chopped parsley**
**1 cup chopped scallions, greens and whites**
**Grated rind of 2 lemons**
**½ cup lemon juice**
**2 teaspoons salt**
**⅓-½ cup olive oil**
**3 tablespoons chopped fresh mint leaves**
**Lettuce leaves**
**Garnish: Black Greek olives; lemon wedges**

Soak the bulgur in cold water for about 30 minutes; it will expand and soften. When it is tender, pour it into a strainer and press out the water. Spread the drained grains on a clean dish towel or piece of cheesecloth and roll it up while preparing the rest of the salad. This will help to dry the bulgur even more, so that it can absorb the lemon juice and olive oil.

Place the chopped tomatoes in a large bowl. Add the chopped parsley and scallions. Grate the lemons before juicing them, and then add both the rind and the juice, along with the bulgur, to the bowl. Add salt. Toss lightly with your hands (it's more ethnic that way). Pour some of the olive oil over the salad, toss with your hands, and add more oil until the grains begin to stick together. Taste and add additional salt and lemon if necessary. Toss with mint leaves just before serving.

It is customary to serve this salad on a bed of small lettuce leaves either on individual plates or on a platter, so that you can roll up the salad in a leaf and eat with your hands. Garnish the plate with black Greek olives and thin wedges of lemon.

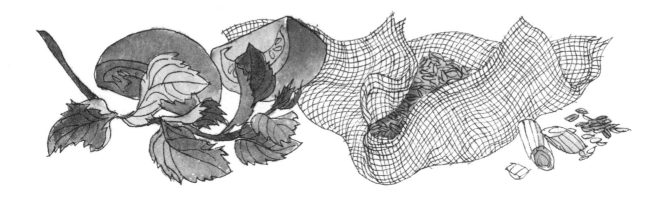

# Pasta Salad Copenhagen

*In the months I lived in the fairytale city of Hans Christian Andersen, I never saw or ate a pasta salad, but that was before such foods became fashionable. The essence of this salad, however, is indeed Danish, especially in its typically extravagant use of fresh dill. I even remember eating Chinese food in Denmark garnished with that ubiquitous weed!*

**12-16 ounces shell-shaped or
  corkscrew pasta**
**1 pound Danish ham in a single
  piece, or substitute any good-
  tasting boiled ham**
**½ pound Havarti cheese**
**2 green peppers**
**2 sweet red peppers**
**3 cucumbers, peeled**
**2 ripe tomatoes**
**1-1½ cups Vinaigrette (see page 55)**
**5 tablespoons chives**
**4 tablespoons fresh dill or
  2 tablespoons dried dill weed**
**Salt and pepper to taste**

Bring about 4 quarts of salted water to a boil (add 1 teaspoon salt per quart). Add the pasta and disregard any cooking instructions on the packet. There is only one way to know if the pasta is done, and that is to taste it. When making a pasta salad it is important to remember that the dressing will act on the pasta exactly as a marinade acts on fish or meat—it's going to break down its texture. So the pasta will be ready when it is barely tender and still *quite* firm. This may take as little as 1 minute for fresh pasta or as little as 4 minutes for dry pasta. Drain the pasta and submerge it in cold water to stop the cooking and cool it. When it is completely cold, drain it well.

Slice the ham, cheese, green and red peppers and peeled cucumbers into pieces just slightly larger than your little finger. Cut the tomatoes into wedges. Toss all these ingredients in a bowl with the drained cold pasta. Pour in the vinaigrette and mix with your hands. Add the chives and dill and season with salt and pepper. Let the salad stand at room temperature for 30 minutes before serving to allow all the flavors to blend. Taste before serving and add more herbs and salt and pepper if you wish.

NOTE: The ingredients in this salad can be varied to create almost endless combinations. Try pieces of tongue, Jarlsberg or cheddar cheese, blanched green beans or asparagus.

# Moroccan Rice Salad

*When Paula Wolfert came to teach at my cooking school, the students quickly became intoxicated with her spell-binding cooking aromas. The smells of roasting peppers, cumin and preserved lemons, and cinnamon and orange water left us absolutely smitten. This salad was inspired by her class.*

**2 cups raw rice, cooked and cooled
  (see page 13)
2 fresh red peppers, roasted (see
  page 15), or 4 canned pimientos
1 head iceberg lettuce
½ sweet white onion, finely chopped
  (see page 14)
1 handful fresh parsley, chopped
½ cup pitted black olives, sliced
½ cup green olives, sliced
½ cup heavy cream
2 tablespoons olive oil
2 tablespoons white wine vinegar
1-2 tablespoons cumin
1-2 tablespoons curry powder
¼-½ teaspoon cayenne
Salt and freshly ground pepper
  to taste
12 large shrimp, cooked (see page
  15), or 2 cups cooked and cubed
  chicken (optional)**

Cook and cool the rice. Meanwhile, prepare the remaining ingredients. Dry the peppers or pimientos on a paper towel, slice in thin strips and mince. Cut the lettuce in half through the core and remove the core. Shred the entire head into a chiffonade. Put the peppers, lettuce, onion, parsley and olives in a very large bowl.

Whisk together the cream, olive oil, vinegar, cumin, curry powder and cayenne in a 2-quart bowl. Season with salt and pepper.

Toss the cold rice with the vegetables. Pour on the dressing and toss gently. Taste for salt and pepper again. Refrigerate for 1 or 2 hours so that the flavors can blend. Taste before serving to adjust the flavor. Serve on a large platter piled in a pointed mound to resemble the lid of a Moroccan *tagine*.

NOTE: To turn this salad into a main course simply add the shrimp, cut in half lengthwise, or add the chicken.

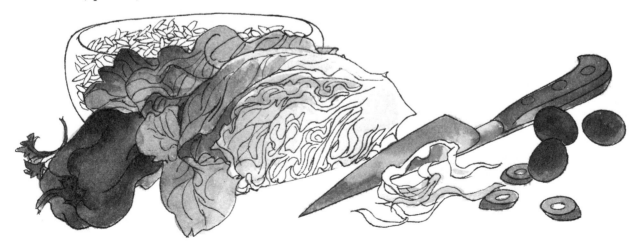

# HAPPY MARRIAGES IN SMALL SALADS

Try:

• Sliced tomatoes tossed with watercress and small pieces of raw cauliflower. Dress with lightly curried Vinaigrette and garnish with toasted almond nibs.

• Slices of cucumber and tomatoes dressed with dilled Vinaigrette made with an egg.

• Torn pieces of chicory, thin slices of beets and sections of oranges finished with a red wine Vinaigrette to which you have added a pinch of sugar.

• A bed of Romaine covered with slivers of hearts of palm and sections of grapefruit, tossed with a lemon-and-grapefruit-juice Vinaigrette with a touch of chopped mint.

• Bibb lettuce dressed with sherry vinegar and walnut oil, garnished with toasted walnuts.

• Crunchy leaves of Romaine torn, tossed with slices of avocado, black olives and a Vinaigrette lightly flavored with thyme. Pass freshly grated Parmesan at the table.